Turn Right at Lost

Recalculating America

Rick Elkin

FIRST EDITION

Amelia Painter Press

Turn Right at Lost: Recalculating America
Copyright ©2016 by Rick Elkin

FIRST EDITION
Cover and Interior Design: Graphic Details
Editor: Lindsey H. Boetel

POLITICAL SCIENCE / Political Process / Campaigns & Elections
HISTORY / United States / 21st Century
http://turnrightatlost.com
http://ameliapainter.com

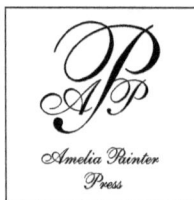

Amelia Painter
Press

Sun City, Arizona

ISBN: 978-0-9969121-2-9
Printed in the United States of America.

First Edition
10 9 8 7 6 5 4 3 2 1

This book is dedicated to my angel,

soul mate and wife, Cathy,

my children Kelly and Jeff,

and to my mom and dad,

for giving me the love to be me.

To Walt Disney for stimulating my latent imagination;

To Ronald Reagan whose inspiration and clarity brought me back from

the brink;

To my old buddies from the sixties who were crazy enough to see the outer

limits,

and to the

United States of America,

our family nest on top of

the Tree of Life.

TABLE OF CONTENTS

Introduction

Come mothers and fathers, throughout the land
And don't criticize what you can't understand
Your sons and your daughters are beyond your command
Your old road is rapidly agin'.
Please get out of the new one if you can't lend your hand
For the times they are a-changin'.

-Bob Dylan

Have you ever been truly lost?

First, you have to have a feeling that something is not right. Then you start looking for some signs of familiarity. You then retrace your steps in your mind or review your directions. What did I miss? Maybe I misread the map, or went left when I should have gone right. Then a creeping sense of panic sets in when you realize none of this looks familiar or proper. The first instinct is to stop. No need to go further and get more lost than before. When you finally give in to the apparent truth that you are actually totally lost, then what? If you can call someone, you will need to tell them where you are for them to be able to help you. If you are totally on your own, out of cell phone coverage, with limited knowledge of the area you have ventured into, just what is the best way to get reoriented?

If you were driving, your GPS would be saying, "Recalculating."

We all know the best way is to retrace your steps. If you know where you came from then you have a good chance of working back into familiar territory. So you turn around 180 degrees and slowly move back in the direction from which you came. Only to the extent that you recognize some sign posts, or you may well be getting so far off the path you will never figure out where to go next. Which is a condition that would require you to simply stay put until some other force or factor discovers you are missing and comes looking for you.

If you have been following American politics the past couple of decades, to even the least observant or engaged citizen, there are increasing signs that our country is lost in the dark woods of discord and conflicting views of who we are and where we are, and where we should be going.

Like voices in the head of a lost hiker, America is conflicted, confused, and increasingly frustrated and angry. Our historical reputation for 'can do' enthusiasm and optimism, is starting to erode.

As we approach the 2016 presidential election, our two party system is starting to look incapable of dealing with the various pressure groups, the economy, and the world's ills. We have a cross section of candidates that paint vastly different pictures of our collective health and happiness.

On the far left, we have a demographic of disenchanted, under employed, and disparate voters who would turn to a Soviet socialist model to redistribute the nation's wealth and hand the job of raising the proverbial children of our society over to big brother. They have been bred to believe they are the most educated and informed generation in world history; they are destined to correct the injustices and hegemony practiced by resource greedy America, once and for all, creating an egalitarian utopia on Earth.

On the far right, we have a strict constitutionalist, evangelical Christian, Texas-styled lawyer who would disassemble the Washington establishment, and reassert states' rights, and give much of the power back to the local levels of government. With a strong influence of biblical morality, he would walk directly back towards the Reagan era model in an attempt to recalculate America, both domestically and internationally.

And then we have a bomb-thrower populist. A sudden, unexpected, and as of now, unexplained attraction that has turned American politics on its ear.

In this historically unique political firestorm voters must decide, are we lost or not? And if we determine we are, what are we, as a nation, going to do about it?

On one side of the ledger, a party wants to elevate and represent an endless parade of tribes. As their leading candidate phrased it, "We need to be tearing down barriers. We don't need to make America great again; we need to make it whole."

"Making America Great Again" as the bomb-thrower on the right slogan suggests would be, presumably, too judgmental. The tribal coalition on the left sees our national condition as broken, run by the top 1% who deny their constituents government programs designed to balance the economic playing field, withhold public support the less 'fortunate' and civil protections for minority rights. Making the country whole again would best be accomplished with a top-down, government-driven agenda of civil laws, PC readjustment of attitudes and social retraining.

The Democratic pledge to help their coalition to gain their share of the pie, to give them government support systems like subsidies, quota systems, separate but equal bathrooms, equality but differentiation, and multicultural identification without integration, draws huge numbers of victims to the voting booth. It has proven to be an effective tool to attract enormous numbers of voters, despite evidence that most, if not all, of their complex and very expensive social programs, which are essentially wealth redistribution programs, don't actually accomplish anything tangible.

On the other side of the ledger, the entrenched, mostly wealthy and comfortable, well-established, deeply religious and patriotic party, though seldom in legislative control, seems to be content with just about everything except every symbolic legislative victory of their opponents. Beyond a loud chorus of bellyaching about health care, excessive federal spending and high taxes, they don't take much time off from the golf course to really accomplish much of anything.

They have become what the original Tea Party rebels hated, an aristocracy of international corporate interests that are too big to fail.

If we didn't know better, we might think this election year is just another reality TV show called 'Animal Farm, USA.' The 4-legged farm animals have become the 2-legged humans.

Suddenly, a TV game show host billionaire comes along and says, "We have to secure our borders. Without borders, we don't have a country. I will build a world class wall. The finest border wall ever built. It will be easy, and I will make the Mexican government pay for it. Aren't you tired of losing at everything?" And with one brilliantly conceived stroke, sucks the air right out of the national campaign room!

The idea that one candidate, by recognizing one issue as the elephant in the room, could have so much impact on the future direction of our country is stunning. But it shouldn't be. Illegal immigration is a microcosm of the problems every industrialized country on the planet is currently, or about to, face. The idea that borders are a thing of the past is so antithetical to the concept of civilization, of law and order, of human dignity, and of national identity, it is counter intuitive. The impact and cost of uncontrolled migration is so enormous and widespread, it fosters a loss of controls of currency, of trade, of cultural identities, and of physical, financial and employment security.

Leaving the doors to our home unlocked is just the beginning of a myriad of cascading problems, all of which are contributing to our nation's political indigestion.

Isn't it poetic justice that a reality TV star, an egocentric real estate developer and author of a business textbook would be the one to slap us collectively across the face to awaken us to the fact that we are truly lost. That his skill set, his highly developed system of recognizing subtle, sometimes subliminal messages would be the only one of hundreds of 'qualified' political leaders to seize on the single mutant cancer cell that is leading us down a dead end road to perdition.

If and when any country loses its identity by abandoning borders, refusing to enforce duly enacted laws, redistributes the hard earned assets of its indigenous citizens, it simply ceases to exist. And along with it goes the human inventory, the entrepreneurship, the initiative to achieve great things and the sense of loyalty and sacrifice any society needs to sustain its viability.

When a soldier is pinned down in a trench and realizes he is about to lose his life, he may ask, for what? For something that everyone on the planet already has? For a lawless, uncivilized country that offers no peace, no justice and no safety for its citizens?

Why not hold up the white flag of surrender and hand over your weapon and your life to your enemy?

Some on the left would say, that's a good idea, we never accomplish anything with war. So, in their mind, we would have been better off had we let Hitler run the table and dominate the world. Or perhaps it would have been Japan, or North Korea, or Russia. The point is, the only ones who ever threaten to run the world are the leftists, the statists, the communists or fascists who think they know better than the average person, and can determine just what we should all be doing in their utopia.

Just ask Napoleon, the Alpha Donkey in George Orwell's *Animal Farm*.

So now is the time to ask: Are we Americans lost? Do we have what it takes to admit our failures while at the same time recognizing what an important and absolutely essential element America plays in the success of civilization on mother earth?

Or are we about to do what everyone did at Orwell's *Animal Farm*, "The animals, watching through the window, realize with a start that, as they look around the room of the farmhouse, they can no longer distinguish which of the card players are pigs and which are human beings."

CHAPTER ONE

Re-Orientating

"We are forlorn like children, and experienced like old men,
we are crude and sorrowful and superficial—I believe we are lost."

— Erich Maria Remarque

My writing journey began on the morning of September 11, 2001.

I woke up to my inner desire to scream. I woke up to the need to be engaged in the future of my country and the world we are leaving for our children. As we were astonished to watch the iconic World Trade Center Towers turn to dust, my kids stood next to me, and I felt the tension in the air, the fear in their hearts. I knew the world would never be the same again...

September 11, 2001, will always be a special day in my life. In everyone's life, there are transformational moments, events that put a new perspective on all that we know. For some of us, it is the birth of our first child. For some, it is graduation day, or a Bar Mitzvah, or a daughter's wedding day.

These are the days of our lives that change our paradigm. September 11, 2001, is a day I can't forget, as much as I would like to...

It isn't a day I want to celebrate, to make music about or to send out greeting cards over. September 11th will always be seared into my mind as the most horrific day I have experienced in my lifetime. That may sound naive to many people. Fighting in a war, or having witnessed a murder or suffered the loss of a young child would be devastating. I have not had such circumstance, so I can't speak to any of those kinds of tremendous emotional nightmares.

Not only did my world change on that September morning, I believe the whole world shifted on its axis. A subtle but transformative shift occurred in both the geopolitical and financial centers of the world, and to a great degree, it changed the trajectory of many of the forgotten corners of the world. Places like Afghanistan, Iraq, Somalia, Yemen and Syria.

I remember saying to my kids, who were slow to come to the TV that morning, "You need to watch this. This may be the most incredible historical event in our lives!" I knew instinctively that this was going to be similar to the attack on Pearl Harbor, "A date which will live in infamy," as then President Roosevelt said.

As the Twin Towers shuddered, as people jumped to their deaths to avoid the torture of fire, as the firemen went up, and finally as the buildings came down, my heart sank.

This was, in my lifetime, the first time I had witnessed my country lose. It lost its iconic image of invincibility, of towering strength and world leadership. It was like watching my dad cry. It hurt me to the core.

Two days later, when President Bush stood on the flattened roof of a New York City fire truck amongst the ruins of the fallen Trade Center and spoke to the tired and heroic first responders, he used a bullhorn to give his speech of appreciation – he struggled to get the horn to work as the crowd yelled, "We can't hear you!"

The President wrapped his arm around a tired and weary firefighter, pulled the bullhorn up to his mouth and said, boldly, " The people that knocked these buildings down will hear all of us soon!"

Boy, did I, and I am sure all of those guys and for that matter, all of the civilized world, need to hear that! I could breathe again! And for the next few years, we Americans started to pull our damaged egos out of the ashes. We started to remember what our role in the world was. We mourned those that were so savagely and undeservedly murdered that day, and we reached out to support our brothers and sisters who lost loved ones too. And it moved us to see most of the world join hands with America.

It didn't matter, at that point, that there were a few crazies who reveled in our losses. We dismissed them as nut cases. Now here we are 15 years later....it hurts again when I see the replays of the Twin Towers collapse.

And the nut cases have expanded exponentially.

What really pains me is the way we, as a nation, have lost our way. How the growing number of left wing nut cases are receiving credibility by many in the media, and even worse, inculcated in our youth by academia. Some search for reasons why, to blame us, to rationalize why some maniacs would justify slaughtering thousands of innocent men women and children, and devastate the lives of thousands of other relatives, fellow Americans, and heroic first responders.

America seems increasingly morally "Lost."

Our emotional bonds have torn, our sense of pride and brother-ship has deteriorated. The world has descended into chaos, and America, and unfortunately a large number of our fellow citizens, have abdicated our leadership role.

September 11, 2001, was a transformational moment in my life and that of our Nation. And when I think back on it, and I think about the world my children are inheriting, I feel like my dad, God Bless his soul, is crying in his grave.

Changing Lanes

I don't remember much of my life before my teen years. I lived in a little house in Altadena California. My parents were hard working, and my dad made time every day to spend a few minutes playing baseball in the street with my brother, myself and our friends. He helped us build a backstop out of old fencing. We mounted it on roller skates so we could wheel it to the side of the street when cars drove by.

I do remember that our family bonded by eating dinner every night together, a tradition I have slavishly tried to maintain. We would also sit in front of our 7 inch black and white RCA TV set on Sunday nights and watch Lassie, Walt Disney and The Ed Sullivan Show. Those moments gave me an enduring love of music, comedy and live entertainment. My first dog was named Lassie, after the TV show star dog that gave me a respect for pets and the relationship we have as their guardians.

Every Sunday night, our entire family would gather around the small television screen to enjoy the family adventures of Lassie, the wild and exciting imagery of Walt Disney's heroes of the Old West Frontier and Adventureland. Then Ed Sullivan would hold court with an unbelievable parade of all kinds of entertainment, from circus acts to the Philharmonic Orchestra.

Those family traditions formed habits in my life that have later turned into numerous game-changing moments.

When I was five, my parents took my ten-year-old brother and me to the newly opened Disneyland Adventure Park. That day may have been the most influential and transformative day in my life.

I drove the cars in Autopia and fell in love with the automobile. I rode in the submarine in A Thousand Leagues Under the Sea and climbed the massive oak tree in Frontierland. I imagined myself as Daniel Boone, a leader of men.

When I came home I immediately started building my miniature version of Disneyland, and the Matterhorn, in a corner of our yard. Months later, as my development expanded, my Dad suggested I should buy the property from him. So he and I entered into my first real estate transaction. Later, when I was ten, and he sold the house, he invested my portion of the equity in a trust fund, set up for my college education. Another major lesson in life, my first return on investment.

I am certain that Walt Disney was the single most influential person, other than my Dad, in my life. Disney taught me how to use my imagination. He made everything seem possible. His only goal in life, it seemed, was to make the planet a better place, and to make people happy.

He built, "The Happiest Place On Earth".

At five years old, I was an original member of the Mickey Mouse Club. I would race home from school to watch Annette Funicello and the Mouseketeers sing and dance and make believe. It is not a stretch to say I later married my childhood sweetheart Annette because my wife Cathy has dark curly hair and a fantastic, positive and happy disposition.

Nearly three decades later, the subliminal memory of Annette Funicello was a game changer for me. Indirectly, Walt Disney had helped me determine my life partner. But Disney had many layers of impact on my life. I have subsequently had an overactive imagination. I have an innate ability to see things in three dimensions, to visualize shapes and spatial relationships. I believe those skills developed as a result of my fascination with how Disney embraced "Imagineering" and the idea that anything was possible.

One day I saw a new guy on The Milton Berle Show on TV. He sang "Hound Dog" and it knocked me out. I was six, but I had a good sense of talent, and I was a bit of a ham. I began to imitate this guy around the house. My folks would call me out when they had friends over for cocktails. They would say, "Hey, Ricky, show our friends your Elvis Presley routine!"

I would play air guitar and gyrate my legs and hips. They loved it! Elvis became my idol. I will never forget when in his first full-length movie, he died. I felt crushed. As the years went by, I turned my afternoon TV attention to Soupy Sales, and I could do a pretty good imitation of Soupy's goofy puppet White Fang.

The point is I am literally a child of the television revolution. My entire existence has been heavily influenced by the presence of a multifaceted electronic box that exposed me to most of those transformative moments in my lifetime. TV changed my life forever, many times over.

If driving while texting is recognized as an extremely dangerous and distracting activity, I think it fair to say that watching TV, and using it as the main source of information, is an equally dangerous way to navigate your life. The information is vital, but the process can be dangerously deceiving.

In the new normal world of digital information and entertainment overload, the average person is easily overwhelmed. Whether we want to admit it or not, we are all grasping for a virtual umbilical cord to reattach to a childlike sense of our mother's secure embrace.

In fourth grade, we had just moved. I was a fish out of water. It was early in the new school year, and I had a tall, bombastic teacher who loved to tease her pupils. In the morning, she would greet us by walking from one side of the classroom to the other while dragging her long, painted fingernails across the blackboard. The "screeeeeeaach!" sound was painful! But it got our attention. Her name was Mrs. Bertozzi, and I was a little intimidated by her.

One very warm day at the end of recess, after ten minutes of intense dodgeball, some students were waiting to get a drink at the water fountain. We were short on time to get back into the classroom. A new friend of mine was taking a long sip. He was very big for a fourth grader and was sweating profusely. Mrs. Bertozzi stood by, then suddenly leaned into the drinking fountain and said, "Hurry up fat boy. You can't drink it all!" I was next in line, but I in shock. That isn't right. The kid was clearly upset and ashamed, but it was the teacher who should have been.

I went home and told the story to my dad. He said, "What do you want to do about it?"

We went to see the principle and I explained my concerns, that teachers shouldn't be abusive, and that she didn't have to disparage his weight. The principal said he agreed and that the issue would be taken up with Mrs. Bertozzi in complete confidence. My dad was very proud of me.

I later found out that Mrs. Bertozzi was very cozy with the principle -- if you know what I mean. It was a rude awakening, a transformative moment, if you will, for a 4th grader.

Since that day, I have been forever suspicious of tall, attractive women and authority figures. I think that was a seminal moment that infused me with a lifelong sense of justice. We hear the term "fairness" a lot in our social discourse. It is indigenous to America to support and promote fairness. As I age, however, it appears to me that the concept of fairness is becoming subjective. Special interest groups use the idea as a crutch to achieve advantages, not just equality. What is fair for one is not always fair for another, mostly because of legal definitions.

In my mind, fairness is not subjective. In its purest form, it is either a win/win, or it is not. Pure and simple. When I see a clear case of something that is unfair, I am motivated to fix it. It is organic; sort of a guy thing if you will.

So if you want to know why I write what I do, now you know.

End of Innocence

As I have related this innocent and yet sardonic story many times, I am sometimes ashamed of myself.

It was a Friday, a parent/teacher conference day at my school. I was thirteen, and since students were excused from classes, my friend and I decided to play golf. I can't for the life of me remember how we got onto one of the most private golf courses in the area, but we were walking around on this beautiful morning, hacking golf balls all over the place.

One of my many errant drives took me a fairway over, and as I passed a group of maintenance workers, I noticed them moaning in pain, huge tears streaming down their faces. They were huddled under a tree around a small transistor radio. As I got closer, I heard "President John F. Kennedy has been pronounced dead!"

I picked up my golf ball and ran back to my friend. "We need to go! Something really bad has happened. I think the President died!" He looked at me incredulously, and we took a direct path to the course entrance.

It was common in 1963 for 13 year-olds to hitchhike (imagine that!) so within minutes we were picked up by a woman who was obviously very distressed.

"Did you guys hear the news? President Kennedy has been shot by an assassin!"

I told her what I had seen. She wanted to know where we wanted to go. We had made arrangements to be picked up later at the nearby shopping center, so she let us off right in front of the Safeway store

As we sat on the curb, a large delivery truck pulled up, and the driver unlocked the newspaper rack and filled it with a stack of freshly printed afternoon editions of the Los Angeles Times.

"KENNEDY DEAD!" was the huge block print headline.

I walked over and put a quarter in, and then, impulsively, took out the entire stack, maybe 50 papers. "What are you doing?" my friend asked. "We're going to spread the word," I replied. Then, I told him to take half and go to the east entrance of the parking lot. I would go to the west end.

We simply held them up to drivers who would roll down their window and hand us a dollar. Within 30 minutes we had sold them all.

Yeah, I know, they weren't ours to sell. I rationalize it this way; if those people had kept those newspapers, they would probably be worth a hundred times more than that today!

Though we went home that evening with a pocket full of money, I will never forget that day or the following funeral and national mourning. I lost my innocence that day in more ways than one.

When I tell this story, people often say, "That's sick! You capitalized on a tragedy!"

True, but I was thirteen and emotionally disturbed. The shock had damaged my ability to process the information, to react in a rational way.

I was old enough to have a sense of admiration and love for JFK. He was our President. He was energetic and inspirational. President Kennedy was special.

Plus, I witnessed the anguish and pain the entire nation was experiencing. Everyone was emotionally crushed. Then, just a few days later, most of us witnessed the murder of Lee Harvey Oswald on live TV. Suddenly, we were not only sad; we were afraid. This was really bad!

That was a transformative moment for a whole generation. The whole country lost its innocence that day in November 1963.

Speed Bumps

When President Barack Obama was elected, most of the nation was energized. Many were elated that a man of color could ascend to the presidency of the most powerful nation on Earth. It was another national transformative moment.

What are transformative moments?

"Transformative moments are those unique points in an individual, an organization or a human system's development, where the conditions for change are very ripe. A transformative moment is a particular confluence of conditions that make rapid, profound growth possible.

Many of us sense that collectively we humans are facing a time of enormous potential. These transformative moments are situations of tremendous potential. Like bifurcation points in complex systems, these situations inherently have multiple paths forward, only some of which fully realize this potential. Many of us sense this is a time of great potential, in our individual lives, in our organizational and social systems – in the human family."

—Geoff Fitch, January 2008

The country, our place in history, our collective cultural experience since 2008 was changed dramatically. That may happen every presidential election, to some degree or another, but in 2008, something very different happened, and history took a turn at a fork in the road.

On a personal level, there have been many such transformative moments. Recalling, reviewing and sharing these game-changing times in our lives is, well, let's say interesting. But for now, let me ask you a few questions, just to get the ball rolling:

Since 2008:

- Have you or someone you know lost their job?
- Do you know someone who has declared bankruptcy or lost their home to foreclosure?
- Have you been angered by the flood of cheap foreign-made products killing jobs in America?
- Do you have more or less disposable income?
- Have you been bothered by over-reaching or conflicting regulations or rules?
- Have you been witness to or experienced sexual harassment?
- Do you feel more or less comfortable in the workplace environment?
- Do you pay more or less for food?
- Do you enjoy discussing politics with friends and neighbors?
- Are you frustrated by conflicting, confusing and downright stupid legal rulings and regulations that just get worse and never seem to get fixed?
- Have you had a child denied advancement to provide an immigrant a "leg up"?
- Have you been afraid to express your faith at work or to friends?
- Are you more or less proud to be an American?

Just wondering....

If you had to guess;

- Has the stock market and Wall Street been more or less stable?
- Has the number of small business start-ups grown or shrunk?

- Has the number and cost of liability litigation gone up or down?
- How about workplace conflict litigation?
- Do most college graduates find work in their field?
- Do unionized government employees get better benefits than private sector employees?
- Is our national economy and the general business climate healthy or unhealthy?

So, what will it take before you decide to stand up and say something about how so many traditionally common, everyday freedoms, assumptions, and activities are no longer part of the American way?

When will you stand up and declare your anger over the demise of the American Dream?

- Will it be when you and your children are forced to move into a mobile home?
- Will it be when there are widespread blackouts that destroy food and drug supplies?
- Will it be when your property is vandalized because you have a flag in your window?
- When you are denied lifesaving drugs because you are too old?
- When you have to boil water to drink it?
- When crime becomes an acceptable survival strategy?
- When you are confined to a state mental institution because your life savings are gone?

I am not trying to be an alarmist. OK, maybe I am.

I find it alarming that so few Americans are alarmed. So many people seem to be living in a bubble, ignoring the world around them. I hear it often; "I don't read or watch the news, it is too depressing and negative."

They have constructed a virtual world where they can remain above the fray, project a happy face, and simply go along to get along. People who are doing well don't want to deal with those who are not. That would be a "buzz kill." Those who are not doing so well are too proud to say so. They are not looking for handouts. They just accept that this regressive social condition is the new normal.

I get that. It is unhealthy to let yourself stress too much. We all need to remain positive. But I also believe that it is unhealthy to lie to yourself. To rearrange reality to suit your desires. That is delusional.

Besides, whether you like it or not, those transformative moments will sneak up on you. They may be enormous changes in climate, international conflicts, or just a fleeting moment when you realize your employer is going out of business, or your children are moving somewhere else because of the high cost of living.

Most of the game-changers in our lives are things we have absolutely no control over. In this book, I will explore some of my transformative moments. But my hope is that it will spur your memory and imagination too.

Transformative moments are like speed bumps on the road of life: you can either blast over them and hope you don't blow a tire or bust a shock absorber, or you can slow down, take them in stride, and move on to live to tell about the experience another day. Either way, it is important that you have correct directions or at least a good idea of where you are going. Even then, it sometimes requires acute awareness and flexibility to get there safely.

America is our collective home. As we traverse the planet, we need to be assured that home will be there when we return, or at least when our children take over.

No one wants to be confronted with the returning soldier syndrome where the home he left in no way resembles the home he returned to.

The Oh Well Generation

"All animals are equal, but some animals are more equal than others."

Comrade Napoleon - *Animal Farm*

In his classic and prescient books *Nineteen Eighty-Four* and *Animal Farm*, George Orwell describes how Marxism disguised as Socialism slowly herds the unknowing and unengaged populace into a trap.

As a reminder, a little over thirty years after the year 1984, borrowing from Orwell and others, and exercising artistic freedom, I thought it appropriate to re-write a little *Animal Farm* history:

Since 1984, while working on their *Animal Farm*, the owners, Mr. Sinclair and Mr. Orwell, were raising sheople. For the most part, sheople are docile, productive farm animals. The farmers were determined, however, to control their natural instinct to roam.

The animal farmer's learned how to control the sheople by finding a comfortable place in their environment and providing cheap, gratuitous entertainment. The sheople couldn't resist it and began to line up every day to be entertained.

Once they were coming every day, the farmer's put a fence down one side of the place where they got their daily dose of escapism. When the sheople got used to the fence, they resumed looking at their entertainment, and the farmers put up another side of the fence.

After a while, the sheople got used to that and went back to their escapist TV, video games, pornography, movies, and psychedelic music, etc. Eventually, the farmers had all four sides of their little world fenced up with a gate in the last side.

The sheople, who were mesmerized and addicted to the entertainment, started to enter through the gate to get more of it. Suddenly, the farmers slammed the gate on them and caught the whole generation of sheople farm animals by surprise.

Sadly, the poor sheople had lost their freedom. They looked at each other in disbelief. They screamed at each other, each blaming the other for not paying attention.

For the next several years, they ran around and around inside the fence, extremely frustrated, as they could see all kinds of interesting things outside of their fence, but the gate remained locked. They bitched and moaned, but they were caught.

They had sacrificed their freedom for simple pleasures.

Soon they went back to entertaining themselves on mind-numbing alcohol, sex and morbid electronic media. Their anger increased, and they grew mentally and physically unhealthy because of their reckless self-indulgence, so the farmers offered them drug therapy to help them feel better. Eventually, the sheople became so used to their routines that they had forgotten how to think for themselves.

Meanwhile, through that same entertainment media, the farmers continually reminded the sheople of how lucky they were to have keepers who understood and felt their pain.

Now, in 2016, the sheople have accepted their fate and believe they are better off in captivity because it is too hard to live in freedom and they are quite satisfied because their brains and their ambition have atrophied.

Amazing, isn't it, in just over 30 years since the last 'New World', thanks to the benevolent keepers at the Animal Farm, we are living in another 'new world.'

In 1949 George Orwell picked the year 1984 as the setting for his iconic novel because he thought it represented a time in the future, not too far away, but enough to be considered a little unpredictable.

The idea of *Nineteen Eighty-Four* was to project, by logical extension, what would happen if the tendencies of his era were to continue to escalate. And the tendencies that worried Orwell were the same tendencies we are seeing amongst inattentive, lazy, self-absorbed and vacuous American citizens, who should, but don't indicate they do, know better.

I call it the "Oh Well" generation.

As described by Wikipedia, I have taken the creative liberty to make just a few minor changes in the wording, just to illustrate my point:

> "*Nineteen Eighty-Four* is a dystopian novel by George Orwell published in 1949. It unfolds in a world of perpetual war, omnipresent government surveillance, and public manipulation, dictated by a socio-political system euphemistically named 'Progressives' under the control of a privileged inner party elite that persecutes all individualism and independent thinking as 'extremist rhetoric'.
>
> The tyranny is epitomized by Brother Obama, the quasi-divine party leader who enjoys an intense cult of personality. Brother Obama and the progressive wing of the Democratic Party justify their oppressive rule in the name of a supposed greater good."

In 1949, Orwell was concerned about post-war nihilism. People were becoming increasingly oblivious to politics because they had had enough of conflict, sacrifice and internationalism. Europeans and Americans had turned inward and were growing more and more self-absorbed.

Does that sound familiar?

I recently watched Megyn Kelly of Fox News, interview the infamous ultra-liberal tenured professor from Northwestern University, a "reformed" American terrorist from the sixties and seventies, professor Bill Ayers. He personifies the way the left rearranges history and reinvents the language to avoid reality.

This guy, and many of his comrades from the '60s group Students for a Democratic Society, have become college professors and spokesmen for the left (or as they like to call themselves 'Progressives').
Ayers is a professor at a major publicly funded college. He is spewing his kind of convoluted, seriously flawed form of indoctrination to young, easily influenced and vulnerable students. And he is far from the exception, but unfortunately in today's climate, his political mentality is the rule on many, if not most, American college campuses.

As did the leaders in Orwell's *Nineteen Eighty-Four*, in his interview with Kelly, Ayers had a convenient "angle" to rationalize what any clear thinking person would call violent, destructive and completely self-aggrandizing "protests" that only a delusional extremist could justify in American politics.

He simply rewrote the history.

Here is the technique utilized by the left: when you are confronted with a contradiction or failure, choose another public figure to use as a foil. Point out how much further to the left or right they are than you, and suggest by attacking your view, that a journalist is being narrow-minded, hateful and partisan. Thus shifting the focus back onto the interviewer, and making yourself look moderate, open-minded and fair.

Or, simply deny you had anything to do with it, characterize the charge as partisan, hateful, and extremist. Ergo, your position is the moderate one and those people, those extremists, are dangerous!

This has been the strategy used by President Obama. I wonder where he learned that technique? It fits right in with comrade Saul Alinsky's infamous book *Rules for Radicals* where Alinsky spells out the exact dogma employed by Ayers and Obama. You may recall that both Alinsky and Ayers played prominent roles in the development of the then young community activist named Barack Hussein Obama.

To achieve their overall goal of tearing apart the pillars of freedom that stand in their way to convert America to a statist-style government, here are the main strategic points of attack leftists like Ayers repeat in lock-step:

- Destroy the family unit; it is the basic foundation on which America has established its worldwide dominance.
- Destroy Christianity; state-ism cannot compete with a belief system that worships a supreme being or any other authority.
- Demonize capitalism; establish a national guilt trip that presents capitalism as selfish, oppressive and destructive.
- Redefine language; through intimidation and exploitation of children and the underclass, progressives can change attitudes and perceptions, and garner emotional support for their effort to reconstruct history and society.

- Multiply and divide special interest groups; agitate and organize angry, disenfranchised minority groups and then pit them against each other and the establishment; then ride in to rescue selected parties and form disruptive and vocal coalitions to defeat conservatives and moderates.
- Rewrite history; destroy any allegiance to the "glamorized" history of the country, remove any incentives to sacrifice oneself for the good of the evil establishment.
- Embrace mother nature and demonize others as agents of destruction; environmentalism is the new religion, which justifies nearly any means to save the planet! Any campaign that engenders extreme emotional energy is good for earth, but bad for individualism and greed.
- Pretend to hate government; while raging against government invasions of privacy such as the IRS, NSA, CIA, or even private efforts to collect data such as Facebook and Google.
- Increase the size and scope of government exponentially; the theory is that if people are working in government, then government can do no bad. Also, government jobs that earn excessive salaries, and offer early retirement and lifetime benefits for doing nothing, are achievable by everyone as long as we all share in the spoils!
- Focus on institutes of higher learning; American schools honor the sanctity of "Academic Freedom" so with tenured service, scholars can establish their own curriculum, especially since college campuses are often isolated, closed societies where political activities can be disguised as a search for truth.
- Control the media; a lesson learned from the Nazi's. People don't know what they don't know, so controlling the

dissemination of information is seminal to obtaining and managing social obedience.

- Reorganize and dominate the legal system; what you can't gain through the popular vote, you mandate through the court system. To do that, you must win the emotional side of the judicial court. This is accomplished by setting precedents that fair is morally superior to right. Right is a subjective, religious based principle, while fair is a universal humanist position that is immutable. Over time, results can be obtained as the judiciary is slowly turned over to the well-educated students from advanced indoctrination centers or what is commonly referred to as law school.

Today, America faces an institutional attack on, and the breakdown and perversion of, traditional home and family bonds; the demonization and attempted eradication of religion to make room for secular political cult worship, as realized by the sycophantic media worship of President Obama. The leaders on the left use the calculated and coordinated manipulation of language and history to advance the agenda of their progressive worldview, and they use deliberate economic strangulation to ensure compliance in the population.

As the strength of our economy continues to weaken, Progressives blame capitalism, corporate greed, institutionalized racism, sexism, and religion-driven hatred and discrimination for all of their failed wealth redistribution schemes such as the public school system and Obamacare.

This is pure Communist dogma!

For example, Democrats characterize the conflict over the abandonment of the security of our borders as "anti-immigration" bigotry, when in fact it is a battle over the proper enforcement of our existing laws.

Democrats characterize those who would object to the government using their tax dollars to fund abortions as a war on women when in fact it is a battle over the sanctity of human life and the moral imperative to defend the defenseless.

When it is difficult to gin up support for your position on a subject, sometimes it is just easier to change or redefine the subject than to factually change minds.

Orwell predicted that State-ism would resort to language manipulation to reorder history and cover up their true desire for control. So today we have multiple news channels all using different terms to speak to their audience, each suspicious of the other because the news coverage appears to be diametrically opposed.

Our major institutions of learning have been overrun by ultra-liberal administrations made up of displaced, disgraced politicians, community organizers and social misfits. With their lifetime tenure, six-figure salaries, and protected status they are free to indoctrinate the next generation of leaders. Bill Ayers is just one of many including Saul Alinsky, Dana Cloud and Ward Churchill, just to name a few of the more well-known radically left leaning "scholars."

There are hundreds. In fact, David Horowitz, a former liberal who turned right, wrote a book about them, *The Professors: The One*

Hundred Most Dangerous Professors in America. Anyone who has college aged children and is concerned about the future of our country and the institutionalization of left-wing ideology in our schools should read it.

Today, one need only examines the regimes of Stalin, Pol Pot, Mao Zedong and Kim Jong-un to see examples of Orwellian dictatorships where atheism and state-worship were forcibly substituted for religion, the deliberate starvation of all but the most elite members of society, and even Orwell's nightmarish vision of children spying on their parents for the state.

In America, we have admittedly minor league versions of these perversions, with children suing their parents for their emancipation, women claiming that birth control restrictions are a war on their health, being perpetrated by religious zealots, and elementary school children being asked to discuss their parent's environmental beliefs.

We have an entire generation of laborers being pushed aside by illegal immigrants who have been purposely imported to gain control over massive numbers of displaced, undereducated and non-unionized workers and to simultaneously bribe the exploited immigrants for their votes.

Orwell uses the book to attack the intrusiveness and arrogance of big government, and inadvertently predated the William Snowden, NSA, CIA, IRS and ICE scandals currently plaguing the ultra-liberal Obama regime.

Like the authorities in *Nineteen Eighty-Four* the current administration careens from crisis to crisis, drumming up fear and anxiety, and by promising to look out for the little guy, continues to grab even more power and create even larger constituencies of mind numbed, economically distracted and drugged voters who have no core values left to defend.

What is most disturbing being that these systemic attacks, besides being foretold in Orwell's book, have all been well documented and investigated, both by government and by investigative journalists for five decades, yet the institutionalized efforts to destabilize our democracy continue unabated!

Now we have a president who refuses to refute many of these issues because he is a closet Alinskyite. We have reached a threshold that may portend the unthinkable, the complete implosion of the American Dream!

Sheep's Clothing

As a part of their aspirations to destroy, or at least redefine America as we know it, here are some of the stated goals of the American Communist Party as told by a former member to Congress during an investigation of un-American activities in the early '60s.

As you read them, think of how many have already become the "new normal."

- Do away with loyalty oaths.
- Capture one or both of the political parties in America.
- Use technical decisions of the courts to weaken basic American institutions, by claiming their activities violate civil rights.
- Gain control of the schools. Use them as transmission belts for Socialism, and current Communist propaganda. Soften the curriculum. Gain control of   teacher's associations: Put the party line in textbooks.
- Use student riots to foment public protests against programs or organizations which are under Communist attack.
- Infiltrate the press. Gain control of book-review assignments, editorial writing and policymaking positions.
- Gain control of key positions in radio, TV & motion pictures.
- Control art critics and directors of art museums. Promote ugly, repulsive, and meaningless art.
- Eliminate all laws governing obscenity by calling them "censorship" and a violation of free speech and free press.
- Break down cultural standards of morality by promoting pornography, and obscenity in books, magazines, motion pictures, radio and TV.
- Present homosexuality, degeneracy, and promiscuity as "normal, natural, and healthy."
- Infiltrate the churches and replace revealed religion with "social" religion.
- Discredit The Bible and emphasize the need for intellectual maturity, which does not need a "religious crutch."
- Eliminate prayer or any phase of religious expression in the schools on the grounds that it violates the principles of separation of church and state.

- Discredit the American Constitution by calling it inadequate, old-fashioned, out of step with modern needs.
- Discredit America's founding fathers. Present them as selfish aristocrats who had no concern for the "common man".
- Belittle all forms of American culture and discourage the teaching of American history on the ground that it was only a minor part of the big picture.
- Support any socialist movement to give centralized control over any part of the culture such as education, social agencies, welfare programs, mental health clinics, etc.
- Discredit and eventually dismantle the FBI, CIA, and all institutions of intelligence gathering.
- Infiltrate and gain control of big business and all unions.
- Treat all behavioral problems as psychiatric disorders which no one but psychiatrists can understand or treat.
- Dominate the psychiatric profession and use mental health laws as a means of gaining coercive control over those who oppose our (Communist) goals.
- Discredit the family as an institution. Encourage promiscuity and easy divorce.
- Emphasize the need to raise children away from the negative influence of parents. Attribute prejudices, mental blocks and retarding of children to suppressive influence of parents.
- Create the impression that violence and insurrection are legitimate aspects of the American tradition; that students and special-interest groups should rise up and make a "united force" to solve economic, political, or social problems.

My point is, whenever you hear Progressives espouse their agenda, or attack their opposition, be sure to place their arguments in perspective of any one or more of the above communist inspired strategic plans designed to tear our country apart. Beware of the wolf in sheep's clothing.

Common Ground

"The happy truth is that conservatives and liberals can share a lot of common ground if they are allowed to do so. If you can read my ideas, and not reject them immediately because I am a liberal, we might be able to celebrate that common ground."
                                                    - Unknown Liberal Writer

Recently, we are hearing the term "common ground" or "common good" bandied about in relation to social unrest, women's' rights, animal rights, cutting military expenditures, expanding educational subsidies, immigration rights, and controlling what we eat and how we recreate. It is used as the justification when Democratic leadership is trying to raise taxes or fees (which is all of the time) or when they are trying to add more layers of regulations and nanny-state controls, all of which are paid for straight out of our pockets.

President Obama was quoted (italicized comments by the author):

"Some people who just control enormous amounts of wealth (class envy), we don't resent their success. On the other hand, just as a practical matter, you're going to have problems making sure we're

investing enough (redistributing wealth) in the 'common good' to be able to move forward. I mean, the fact of the matter is relative to our post-war history, taxes now are not particularly high or particularly progressive (moral relativism) compared to what they were in the late '50s or 60s."

Maybe not, but there is this little thing about discretionary income, the kind nobody has anymore. President Obama ignores the enormous increases in sales taxes (local government demands), business fees passed along as price increases, as well as the enormous burden of legal liability insurance (passed along too) in nearly all segments of the economy. The huge increases in energy costs plus the increasing costs of an advanced education are leaving the lower and middle class with a giant abscess in their budget. And, that doesn't include the newfound costs of President Obama's socialized health care plan.

Liberals always seem to be the ones complaining that conservatives reject their ideas out of hand. My experience is just the opposite. Liberals disrupt, or ban altogether, conservatives from speaking engagements on college campuses all over the country. Conservatives like Karl Rove, Ben Carson, and Rand Paul, have all decided not to appear at commencement speeches because of leftist activism and protests. Activists claim they should not be allowed to speak because they make some students uncomfortable.

It is the activist lefties who interrupt Congress with demonstrations and protests, who orchestrate boycotts against those that they disagree with. Historically, socialists and communist regimes have been responsible for media censorship, mass book burnings and internet interference. It is the liberals who are trying to regulate TV news and radio broadcasts and the world-wide web. They are the ones who bitch about how conservatives rule the airwaves (which is entirely unsubstantiated). They think that the mainstream media is neutral and unbiased because it most closely adheres to their ideology. Liberals see the world as naturally liberal and anyone who is conservative as deviant.

They do not want to listen to the opposition because it is hate filled or misleading.

Their idea of common is not necessarily so common. In fact, as is typical of lefties, they just assume most people agree with their political viewpoint because if you don't, you must be ignorant and retrogressive, so who cares?

This whole notion of "the common good" is a subterfuge for socialism. Please, before you call me a reactionary conservative who doesn't care about anybody but myself, just hear me out.

I remember when I was sharing a house with several other students in college. We had a neat three-story, five-bedroom house just across the street from the beach. We all paid about $250 a month to make the rent. One of the students, whose parents were well off, was able to get his mom to co-sign on the lease guarantee, so he was on the hook if anybody failed to pay their fair share. He was not a student, but he enjoyed having a place to party, so he made the annual commitment. We loved the house so much, we all worked together to make sure we always paid the rent on time. It turned out, that is about all we had in common.

The group was pretty diverse, some were serious students, some were just party animals trying to get through, but not too concerned about school. We decided to take care of our food collectively as I liked to cook and was OK with making a dinner meal every night for all of us. All other meals would be individually taken care of and the food for that, if used in the house, was each person's responsibility (weekend meals were always self-directed). We each had one night a week we were responsible for paying for dinner. That made the other four free, so it was fair.

But it didn't take long for some people to complain that their food was being pilfered. Of course, everyone would deny it, so labels were put on the stuff, but never-the-less, someone was wolfing food they didn't buy.

The other thing we had to decide was how would the kitchen and the house be kept clean? Obviously, if you made something on your own, you were supposed to clean up after yourself. The daily dinners were divided up by day, so everyone had one day of the week they were responsible for washing dishes and cleaning up the house, too. Very egalitarian, right?

But guess what? The kitchen always seemed to be a mess, there were always dirty dishes in the sink, and clothes left around the house, and the floor was always scattered with crumbs and loose stuff.

The bottom line is, not all people have the same values, health habits or disciplines. In the end, we had to put strong controls on anyone who used the kitchen at all. If we found someone was not keeping up or was pilfering other people's food they would either be fined or told to leave.

The "common good" was only as common as each individual deemed it to be, and interestingly, those who promoted "sharing" the most were the same people who actually shared the least. In fact, they were the ones who secretly redistributed others' food to themselves.

So what am I saying? The notion that everybody should carry the weight they are capable of carrying (from Karl Marx, "From each according to their abilities, to each according to their needs") is just an excuse for some people to simply avoid any responsibility.

I'm not willing, nor would you be (I'll bet) willing to put in long hours just to have the majority of my earnings redistributed to someone who is just not motivated to do anything! And no one will convince me that those kind of people don't exist.

One good lesson I took from my college years was that communal living is a hookah pipe dream. Real world experience eventually makes wild-eyed student Marxists into political conservatives. Once they see that paycheck getting pilfered every week, they will change their communal tune real fast.

Road Kill

Another growing cyst in our culture is this crazy idea that we all have to agree. That, like children holding hands in a circle, if we all agree, we can play in harmony. I call it the Rodney King Syndrome; the "can't we all just get along" attitude, which Mr. King coined right after roaming vandals and malcontents had trashed the City of Los Angeles. Rodney, who was filmed fighting with the cops who were trying to arrest him, was later given a multimillion dollar "settlement."

In a speech about economics, listing all of the things he fights for job security, good wages, affordable health care and college educations, reducing poverty and inequality, and of course, increasing opportunities, President Obama also promised to stand up for women's rights, civil rights, the end of war, and most importantly, to fight climate change.

He seemed to be asking, "Can we all just get along?"

He may as well have ended the speech by asking, "Have I missed anything? If I did, it wasn't on purpose. Just let me know what I left out and I'll fix that too!"

President Obama is a poster boy for 21st-century experiments in educating young people. The concept of consensus is endemic to all classroom efforts, to any semblance of debate. In the modern classroom, conflict is forbidden. Historically, elementary school teachers spent a good deal of their time teaching their kids social skills so as to maintain control and to provide a safe learning environment.

Increasingly, though, lessons focus on feel-good subjects focusing on the esteem of the children. The idea is that there are no winners or losers, that every child is special, that all answers have an element of correctness, and that all kids are essentially good. Misbehavior is rendered a symptom, not a trait or anything that can't be fixed with increased levels of love and attention.

The problem with that approach is that misbehavior engenders increased attention, love and benefits for the rascals and as a result, the kids who do behave, are assigned to work with the other trouble makers, making them assistant teachers, and increasing their workload. In the meantime, troublemakers are coddled and pacified, and their work often completed by others. This is a reverse incentive; the incorrigible kids get all the attention, while the hard workers have to work even harder to help maintain any semblance of order.

Parents can be enablers too, because they coddle their kids, want to be their kid's best friends, and will do anything to give them an advantage. They are commonly referred to as "helicopter parents". It occurs to me that politicians in the halls of power, in our legislatures, are "helicopter politicians". They act like elementary school teachers, spending inordinate amounts of time talking down their noses to us, preaching the importance of cooperation and tolerance. When they do legislate, most of it is aimed at protecting one group from another, or to promote a favored behavior or group. They pander to special interests, dishing out rewards for blocks of votes.

President Barack Obama represents the Rodney King Syndrome. In his speech, he was indirectly challenging his audience, "Can't we all just get along?" He reflects a worldview born in the sixties.

Under President Obama, our cultural worldview has rapidly devolved back into that sixties "Love is all we need" mindset:

- Marijuana is a socially accepted recreational drug.
- America is the cause of most of the world's conflicts.
- The police are fascist racists pigs.
- The world is run by a few filthy rich white men.
- Sex is holy and should be free and unrestricted, while taxpayers pay for mistakes.
- Marriage is a construct of repressive males.
- Property belongs to all people and should be equally distributed.
- Education, health care, cell phones, computers and drivers' licenses should be free.

But the ugly truth is that the road kill caused by these misguided ideologies is frightening. It is almost impossible to sit at the dinner table and have a comfortable political discussion, because of "political correctness". The social utopia envisioned by baby boomers as Nirvana has degenerated into cultural confusion and social indigestion.

When large groups of people get together in a park, it is almost always to riot or to battle police, exemplified by Occupy Wall Street and the Black Lives Matter movements. It is near impossible to attend a free music concert without an encounter with police. The drug cartels are hooking up with ISIS and attacking each other, beheading people over marijuana and heroin drug profits. It is dangerous to put a manger display in your yard at Christmas, unless you want your home to get covered in toilet paper or broken eggs. Never put an American flag in the window of your condominium, that will initiate a HOA lawsuit.

If you get married, you will be vilified and made fun of by your friends, and media celebrities. Don't even think about mentioning how that new blouse looks on your secretary because you may be summarily dismissed and sued for sexual harassment.

So, the more things change, the more they do stay the same.

Navigating Cul-de-sacs

Our leaders talk a lot, but the real issues have become road kill, too.

We hear the usual polemic about creating jobs and protecting the less fortunate. Our political parties have the same priorities, national security, family values, education, providing opportunities and bolstering the economy. They just have opposite approaches to the solutions.
Most of the highest profile issues are being dictated by multi-national corporate Super Pac campaign contributions (bribes) and powerful special interest group pressures.

I think the politicians and the media miss the real issues. When they speak of national security, they are talking about funding gigantic government bureaucracies of security guards and paper pushers who harass little old ladies at the airport. Security equates to larger intelligence agencies and vast bureaucracies of airport and public security agents, most of whom have little more than a high school education.

When they orate about education, they are talking about newer schools, more teachers and larger teaching unions and higher salaries.

They are assuming the problems with our educational system revolve around funding.

When I worry about the issues of our educational system, I am referring to specific failures: our children graduate from high school unprepared to handle even the most remedial of life's problems. They can't balance a checkbook, for example. How much do you want to bet, most high school graduates couldn't identify the NYSE. Does your eighteen-year-old know how to fill out his income tax form? Would he/she have any idea about what kind of life insurance or workman's compensation supplemental insurance policies might be important to own at this point in their life?

How about their auto insurance? You know, the policy you have been paying for, that by all rights, they should now take over. Do they understand the language of liability, compensation, and damages?

Let's face it, your child knows more about Lady Gaga, global warming and the politics of self-gratification than you will ever know, but the questions of how to live without mom and dad have, for the most part, never been addressed. They have all the stats and stories about spilled oil, rainforest deterioration and how fossil fuels are destroying the planet, but have no clue about how to invest in an IRA.

This generation acts like they are the first ones to experience everything; the first generation to feel disenfranchised; the first generation to feel the effects of isolation; the first generation to suffer from unfair competition and globalization, to be aware of the destructive forces of the automobile, of eating gluten and wearing leather shoes.

The first generation to have to answer for their decisions.

The politicians, they claim, don't talk about solutions. Instead, they trash their competition. The Congress is a do-nothing body, and the political parties don't listen to the regular people. Young voters are correct; politicians aren't addressing their issues. But they aren't addressing anybody's issues directly! They are working for special interests, not us.

In the area of foreign affairs, the politicians are consumed with power struggles, turf wars and alliances of convenience. Our major political institutions are playing board games based on the roll of the contribution dice. Nothing happens unless the dice are thrown, and the voters are not holding the dice.

Part of the reason the politicians get away with it is the low voter turnout, and their ability to affect outcomes using diversions and payouts to their collective partners, unions, industry, the military, and the media.

The big question is how do voting citizens sort out what is true and what is some construction? What is vitally important and what is some special interest's priority? Because so much of the massive amounts of information we must sort through is constantly redefined and massaged by the media, identifying and defining the real issues is as difficult as addressing them.

George Orwell put it succinctly in his novel *Nineteen Eighty-Four*:

> "He who controls the past controls the future. He who controls the present controls the past."

Control is the keyword; for most of us, that means navigating the cul-de-sac of our neighborhood, our circle of influence, our closest friends and family, and most importantly, our immediate actions. Individually, we must start working close to home to affect change. This is where we the people, those who are driving the agenda of our great nation, have to make the adjustments, where we have to exert our influence, where we have to recalculate our directions, and our future, and that of our kids.

CHAPTER TWO

Illusions

"We all want progress, but if you are on the wrong road, progress means doing an about-turn and walking back to the right road; in that case, the man who turns back soonest is the most progressive."

— C. S. Lewis

Drugs, gambling, sex, and food addictions are well known and fairly common. Society accepts the fact that some people are predisposed to becoming addicted to things. Experts claim a genetic defect is the primary difference between those who can smoke one cigarette a week and those who chain smoke.

Drug addicts, once weaned off drugs, often substitute something else to obsess about. Alice Cooper, the 80's era metal rocker, turned to golf to feed his compulsive need for the adrenaline high he got from cocaine. Addiction therapists say compulsive overeaters are really looking for affection. They soothe their loneliness with a Wendy's triple cheeseburger.

All of this is an attempt to understand why a rapidly growing number of people are in one way or another either dependent on or addicted to something. In fact, I would argue that virtually everyone is hooked on something.

In today's world, we obsess on so many things it is sometimes hard to differentiate one addiction or obsession from another. The obvious clinical dependencies caused by narcotic drugs are only the top of the pyramid. Expanding exponentially below that is a myriad of habits that at some point qualify as addictions, or at best, obsessions.

Since the advent of the internet, sex addictions are growing across all sectors of society, affecting not just the stereotypical "dirty old man" but also creeping into the lives of women and children.

Former President Bill Clinton made light of his compulsion to conquer flirty women. His high-profile fling with a White House intern brought a national epidemic into the spotlight. The fact that he became more popular afterward shows how "normal" is different now than just a generation ago.

A whole generation is facing the challenge of resisting an addiction to personal electronic devices, while losing the ability to establish personal relationships. Excessive online gambling, virtual sex, cyber-bullying, e-commerce spending sprees and general isolation issues are all typical daytime TV talk show topics. It is increasingly difficult to sit in a restaurant without noticing virtually everyone is looking at their cell phones instead of the person they are eating with.

Many women are suffering from eating disorders and self-image hatred and often act out this neurosis with self-destructive and compulsive behaviors. Celebrity publications offer photo spreads of the physical degeneration of models, actresses and media darlings who sometimes succumb to the need to be thin. This is also indicative of our cultural obsession with the destruction of strong personalities; we love to expose their human frailties.

Some would suggest that tattoos and body piercing is a form of self-abuse that hides an underlying anger that engenders itself by using the body to send messages of fear, abandonment and distrust in authority. Many people will tell you that after they became addicted to tattoos, they would often spend food or mortgage money on new tats.

Most compulsive people, unfortunately, are completely unaware that they have any problem at all. Some political activists will give up lucrative jobs, family connections, friends, lovers, and any number of treasured personal items to devote themselves to saving the planet or getting a favored politician elected.

For some, politics is a religion, a management system that requires complete and utter commitment. When the election cycle comes to an end, they are lost souls, so they quickly find a new crusade to join.

Sports and other entertainment can dominate the agenda for many people. Building their entire life experience around the thrill of watching or participating in some form of non-essential, bigger than life activity becomes the driving force in their lives. Similar obsessions can manifest themselves in many ways, such as celebrity stalking, obsessive unrequited love, or an insatiable appetite for pornography, video games, online gambling, sports bookmaking, movie watching, violent, loud and abrasive rock or rap music, and super dangerous extreme sports activities.

For a minuscule percentage of these people, their obsession leads to a business success, which in turn encourages others with similar personality types to enter the fray. Snoop Dog and Bob Marley, musicians who helped make marijuana use commonplace, have made enormous fortunes selling drug paraphernalia.

The huge financial rewards for the top echelon of extreme sports is seductive; the activity, however, becomes habit forming, and though most soon realize they will never accomplish celebrity status, some continue the activity at great financial and physical cost. Thousands of skateboarders, sky divers, mountain climbers and big wave surfers are maimed and killed annually, dreaming that someday they too would be rich and famous.

All you have to do is look at TV Guide to see how the reality show is dominating the schedule of most cable stations. Reality shows are semi-documentary, participatory programs about people with extreme obsessive compulsive behavior patterns. As these programs gain audience share, you could make the case that the audience itself is practicing voyeurism, another form of Addictive Personality Disorder (APD).

In this modern era of multi-media and social network digital communications, the human experience has evolved to include less and less group human interaction, physical work activity and self-reliance. Recent social studies show attention spans have shrunk measurably, and though young people will claim to be good at multi-tasking, studies show that such activity is generally counter-productive at best.

What we are left with is a generation of self-centered, isolated and angry people who have an insatiable appetite for attention, stimulation, approval, instant gratification, and celebrity. We center our lives on a series of illusions, many of which are habit forming, and in too many cases, destructive.

I have always described myself as a student of the media. When I arrived at California State University at Long Beach in 1978, I had no idea what I wanted to do with my life. I was interested in rock and roll and hoochie coo. I just wanted to get a degree and avoid the draft.

So when they asked me to declare a major, I looked around and decided that radio and TV were the most interesting field for me. It was my favorite topic of discussion; it was evolving rapidly and other than that, it wasn't algebra.

I used to tell the story of why I see myself as a child of television. When I was 7 or 8, my dad and I had just watched something on TV. He got up to go get his favorite Hamm's beer. I asked him, "Hey dad, where was I conceived?"

I could see the look of amusement on his face. He must have thought, 'OK, this is as good as any time to have that talk about sex.'

He was walking towards the kitchen, so he paused and looked back at me as I sat cross-legged in front of our TV. "Right there!" he said, nodding towards me. It wasn't until years later that I realized he meant on the sofa. Because at the time, I assumed he meant on the floor in front of the TV. So when I say I have always thought of myself as a child of the TV generation, I really meant I was conceived right under the TV.

Little did I know that there was an umbilical cord attached to me that would follow me, and my baby boomer brothers and sisters around for the rest of our lives.

A Fork in the Road

I was fortunate to stand out in my senior class at California State University at Long Beach (CSULB), so my department head asked me if I would be interested in participating in a post-graduation summer program designed to place graduates in the field of their major. It was not a work placement program or apprenticeship, just a volunteer, unpaid student training program sponsored by the National Academy of Television Arts and Sciences. If I was willing, along with only 4 other students, I could choose my area of interest from a list of participants, and I would spend six weeks following an industry professional around, as he performed his daily tasks.

I was all in.

I was placed with an account manager with the Leo Burnett advertising agency in Hollywood. I would be up close and personal in the development and production of television ads produced by the largest international ad agency in the world!

I always thought the best job in TV would be to create 30 and 60-second ads. In my mind, it affords the most creative license, the widest possible audience, and is constantly changing with social and cultural tides.

On my first day, I was lead into the producer's office on an upper floor of a prestigious office building around the corner of Hollywood and Vine. I waited for a few minutes, and while looking out the window at the parking lot below, I saw a man pull up to a reserved parking spot. He was driving a fire-engine red convertible Austin Healey. He climbed out and revealed his dapper attire, a vest and gabardine slacks over expensive loafers. He wore a derby and had a handle-bar mustache!

I wasn't sure if he was my new mentor, but you couldn't find a more stereotypical Hollywood producer at a casting call.

A few minutes later he appeared in the office and introduced himself as Patrick. He sat behind his enormous desk and asked me to be patient while he set up the day's agenda. He put his feet up on the desk, placed a large tobacco pipe in his mouth, lit it, and began making phone calls.

Around 10:30 he gathered up his leather shoulder bag, and said, "Let's go. We have a busy day, and we can get acquainted on the road!" We spent the day bouncing around from office to office. We stopped at the title company; then we had lunch at Musso and Frank's Grill, where I witnessed a parade of famous actors. Patrick played pool as we waited to see other actors, producers and agents. It seemed every office had a pool table in the waiting room.

I don't know what I learned that day, but I knew one thing for sure; I can do this!

My most memorable experience was the shooting of a pilot ad for Schlitz Malt Liquor. It was the brainchild of a writer from the main office in Chicago, and Patrick was the producer. We had spent lots of time going over the script, selecting locations, and setting up the cast. I got to interview, listen to and evaluate audition readings of the actors.

When the big shoot day came along, Patrick told me to enjoy everything but stay out of the way. It would be a wild and long day, so I was on my own. I could stay for the whole thing or feel free to go home whenever I wanted.

The plot was simple; three guys standing at a bar have just ordered a jumbo sized 16-ounce can of Schlitz Malt Liquor, or as it would soon become known as the "Bull." The idea was that this very powerful, high alcohol content malt liquor would appeal to inner city dwellers because they could get a huge jolt from just one can. So the ad had to convey that and appeal to a broad range of blue-collar workers and poor inner city minorities.

This was a new product category that held a lot of promise and a lot was on the line. If successful, Leo Burnett and the Schlitz Brewing Company could realize millions in sales and ad revenue as the brand grew and additional support ads were ordered.

We had installed a set in an airport hangar at the Burbank Airport. The "bar" was all breakaway furniture. There were twenty separate cameras around the bar room to capture the action. The three actors would stand at the long bar, which concealed a cinder block wall. The bartender would put one can in front of the three guys, and the actors would look at the fellow sitting next to him and say, "I'm not opening that!" while sliding the can down the bar in front of his neighbor, indicating the can held some threatening force. We had selected three very talented actors, one small Jewish 'Woody Allen' type, a large white Polish type, and an even larger 'lineman' type black guy.

Yes, political correctness was just becoming omnipresent in 1972.

After they finally force the little guy in the middle to pop the top (which they shot in ultra-slow motion to highlight the spray and the frost on the can), a pair of wooden bar doors open in the back of the bar and a really, really big black rodeo type bull bursts into the room and demolishes everything. The actors literally dive over the bar (onto strategically located mattresses), and the jingle plays as the bull bucks and kicks every bit of furniture into smithereens.

All of this was incredibly well orchestrated and choreographed. A couple of professional rodeo cowboys were hired to handle the bull. The set was surrounded by a steel fence, so when shooting was over, the bull could be herded back into the waiting panel truck.

One thing I learned that day, among many, was that things never go quite according to plan. The lighting, the timing, the actors and their carefully rehearsed escape over the bar all went perfectly.

Unfortunately, the bull wasn't satisfied with wrecking the set. He decided he wanted to explore the whole hanger, so he just crushed the steel fence like it was made of toothpicks. I was, at that point, hiding up in the rafters as was much of the support crew. Others fled for their lives out a side door, including Patrick.

I relate all this because I was totally enthralled by my experiences. I met celebrities every day and found most to be gracious and humble people. I was involved in nearly every aspect of the production process, from casting to editing. And I was seduced by the exotic appeal of Hollywood. It represented all that was exciting about filmmaking, advertising, and Hollywood.

Well, almost all of it.

After my summer program had ended, I submitted the required report to my department head, and I was done. I graduated and was ready to go get a job in Hollywood.

I went back to the studios, to the production houses, the ad agency, to every facility I had visited. I submitted a simple one-page resume and a letter describing my summer training experience. Everywhere I went, I was treated respectfully, but without exception, I never got a response from any of them.

I was devastated. I was willing to work for minimum wage, to start in the mail room. I knew I had no real world filmmaking experience; I had no relatives in the industry. But I thought the fact that I had worked right alongside a whole host of talent in the field would open some entry level doors.

I got nothing.

By the following summer, I was so far removed from the scene that I was desperate. I went back to the ad agency and asked to visit Patrick. He came down to the lobby and walked outside with me. He said he was ashamed to admit it, but my problem was not about me. It wasn't my lack of experience. He said the truth is if you really want to get started in this business, you will need to go to a small town and hook up with a local TV or radio station.

"Why is that?" I asked.

He said,

"Look, Hollywood is one of the most sought-after industries in the
world. First, everyone who is currently employed has someone they
know, a son or daughter, a brother, or a best friend, who is going to
get helped first. We are very paternalistic. That is just human nature.
Second, the Nixon Administration has issued a quiet but
threatening mandate to the leaders of Hollywood industry; hire
more minorities on your own, or the federal government will be
forced to step in. Speaking for myself, even if I wanted to hire you, I
would have to turn you away because you are a white male. Precisely
the problem, as far as the Administration is concerned, Hollywood
is dominated by white males."

That ended my relationship with the radio and television industry.
I was crushed, but I was not going to move to Podunk Iowa to start
a career. I already had a job; I was working in the ski business, and
having a lot of fun. I wasn't getting rich, but I was living a pretty good
lifestyle, so I had reached a fork in the road.

I had to *recalculate* my future.

It wasn't until many years later that it hit me that I had been a victim
of reverse discrimination. Maybe I was naive, but at that point in time,
I was race blind. I had never had any reason to notice the color of skin,
or the sexual orientation of anybody, especially myself.

I have often wondered where I would be today had I chosen to move
to a small town, to go into the fledgling TV industry. I would have
been at the cutting edge of the explosion of cable, which expanded the

opportunities exponentially. I look at the impact of technology and how unbelievable the world of digital and computer aided production has expanded creative options beyond the most active imagination.

No matter how I look at it, choosing to walk away from Hollywood was a transformational moment. But not working in Hollywood didn't cut my umbilical cord to the TV. In retrospect, it may have saved my life by avoiding what later proved to be the decadent Hollywood lifestyle, but my life has an element of the TV and the media embedded in it simply because I am a product of the television generation, and I am now, and always will be, addicted to it.

Gone Tomorrow

The Seattle grunge group Nirvana had one of their biggest hits with *Smells Like Teen Spirit*. Kurt Cobain, the tragic lead singer and songwriter, committed suicide at the age of 27. I believe he was conflicted by the enormous commercial success of his music. The song, which he described as a diatribe against mass conformity, became the signature identity of Nirvana, even though in his mind it was nothing more than an angry indictment of apathy.

He had no idea that "Teen Spirit" was a cologne marketed to teenage girls. He had simply copied it from graffiti and thought it might translate into a pop song. But it has become a celebration of the grunge movement because the song evokes teen angst, rebellion and a sense of worthlessness and helplessness. One line, in particular, reflects the throwaway nature of our modern society and to predict a dystopian future, and was a phrase Kurt often used when arriving at a party: "Here we are now, entertain us."

If there is one element of western culture that all of us can agree has morphed into an unimaginable monster in the past half century, it is entertainment. What my parents considered entertainment and what is considered entertainment today are diametrically opposed to each other.

In the era before the invention of television, entertainment was mostly live, or to a limited degree, radio or recordings. Reading a book was entertaining, but performance entertainment was generally either musical, spoken, or a circus or vaudeville type show.

Entertainment was saved for special occasions. The average weekday had little room for diversions from work. Not working was very rare, so most of that time was delegated to taking care of family and personal needs. It didn't take much to find some simple forms of entertainment; playing with a harmonica, a yo-yo, some dice, or a slinky for little kids.

Today, things are quite different. Entertainment is available 24/7. It is indigenous to our lives. We eat, drink, and sometimes even sleep with some device delivering music, information, games, news, books, and communications. All of these media are embedded with an entertainment element to draw attention, to gain audience and, of course, to sell us something.

"Here we are now, entertain us."

We all love the recent musical offerings of Beyoncé or Taylor Swift, but the question is will any of this young generation of superstars have staying power? Like some of the currently touring rock bands of the '60's, will the newer ones be touring fifty years from now? No way, because they won't even be around twenty years from now. The market can't wait to discover the next superstar, so it makes the last one irrelevant almost as fast as it made it famous.

"Here we are now..." Gone tomorrow.

Our collective attention span is near zero. We eat up the latest and the greatest (whatever) and are immediately hungry for the next new thing! Our appetite is insatiable. As a child of the television generation, my experience with visual media is very wide and deep. I have watched the TV medium grow from a crude 7" black and white image to 90" 4D OLED high definition, smart digital television with a curved screen and interactive online gaming abilities. I can order my groceries on my TV. I can monitor my baby from my office. I have it on most of the day and night. When I walk I listen to music, when I sit in my hot tub, I dictate blogs. And if that's not enough, I can do that and more on my smartphone!

My kids have been essentially brought up by audio video virtual environments. What they know, or think they know, came to them via some digital device or another. For them, there is no such thing as a library; they just search Google. If there is no visual element to it, they are not interested. They don't read for fun.

There is a new disease, called Functional Digital Incapacitation or FDI. It means people are becoming addicted to electronic input (actually, there is no such medically acknowledged condition, I just made that up. But my guess is there will be soon as the medical industry knows an opportunity when it sees one). The symptoms occur when video game players, or cell phone or notebook users are deprived of a stream of consciousness electronic stimuli, they have convulsions and other symptoms of withdrawal. There is a whole generation that is threatened with a long-term disability caused by too much stimulation of the nervous system. It is an overload that the human body has no defense for.

But young people can't get enough of it because as of right now it is not viewed as a threat. it is viewed as the new normal. It is a high, a virtual narcotic.

And for the most part, it is an illusion.

And then there is the most unique cultural enigma, the unprecedented rate of social, technological and intellectual change. If we look at the information, the technological and the data processing curve during the modern era, the curve has gone from a slow, gradual rate of ascension to nearly straight up. What humans have learned and accomplished in the past one hundred years is one hundred times what we achieved in the previous ten thousand.

Think of how much has changed, how our technology has increased just since 1969 when America put the first man on the moon. I was born in 1950, and TV was just an idea. In just nineteen years, the entire world watched Neil Armstrong step out of a spaceship onto the surface of another planet!

Change is occurring at such a high rate it is causing insecurity. As if the threat of terrorism wasn't enough, we all have to deal with immediate obsolescence as a way of life. No sooner is a great product or idea born then it becomes useless junk. No person or object is safe from being replaced. We are all walking on thin ice all of the time. Whether it is our family and friends, our politics, our belief systems, our jobs or our hairdo, it may be all gone tomorrow.

It is difficult to be honest, consistent, reliable or honorable. It is much easier to be disengaged, noncommittal, unpredictable -- or liberal. It is much easier to agree that the planet needs saving, that everyone should be given a living wage or health insurance. It is much easier to agree with all of the emotional issues of protecting the underprivileged, saving the whales, and making abortion cheap and available.

How can one argue with John Lennon, "Imagine all the people, living life in peace?" Thirty-five years after that song hit the airwaves, it is still an anthem for many. It depicts the utopia realized in our lifetimes. It wonders why do we have the same problems over and over again? It asks why even with all of the dramatic change in our world, why are there still no real answers?

Unknown to most, Lennon privately harbored a very conservative philosophy. He was the son of a middle-class English working man, and he believed in self-sufficiency, less government intervention and private property rights.

If you listen to many of his songs, he reveals his disdain for radicals and malcontents. He resented being resented for his success.

Revolution

You say you want a revolution, well you know
We all want to change the world
You tell me that it's evolution, well you know
We all want to change the world
But when you talk about destruction
Don't you know you can count me out?
Don't you know it's gonna be alright?

You say you got a real solution, well you know
We'd all love to see the plan
You ask me for a contribution, well you know
We're doing what we can

But when you want money for people with minds that hate
All I can tell you is brother you have to wait
Don't you know it's gonna be alright?

You say you'll change the constitution, well you know
We all want to change your head
You tell me it's the institution, well you know
You better free your mind instead
But if you go carrying pictures of Chairman Mao
You ain't going to make it with anyone anyhow
Don't you know it's gonna be alright

In a 2010 article in *Vanity Fair* by David Camp, discussing Lennon's application to become an American citizen, Lennon revealed that he would cast his vote in the '84 presidential elections for Ronald Reagan.

"I think we're at a point where there's too much government in everyone's business and too many people looking for handouts... My father was a merchant seaman who walked out on the family. He couldn't be bothered with me until I was a rich Beatle, and then he was suddenly comin' round all the time, hat in hand. That's where we're at with America, you know—people knocking on Uncle Sam's door, hands outstretched, [doleful voice] 'Help me, man. Gimme, gimme.' Ronnie, he understands that it's time to bloody slam the door."

Camp wrote:

"The public response was apoplectic, with protesters making bonfires of Beatles records (again) and Jann Wenner (publisher of Rolling Stone magazine) placing his famous 'Dear John' letter on the cover of Rolling Stone, accusing Lennon of undoing a legacy of peace and music for a few tax breaks and announcing that thereafter, Lennon—who had been the cover boy of *Rolling Stone's* very first issue—would never again see his name in the magazine's pages".

The left felt betrayed. *Rolling Stone* magazine censored John Lennon! A classic example of reverse diversity and the "open mindedness" so often claimed as the exclusive property of the left is simply an illusion.

My point is most of what we see in the world of entertainment is an illusion.

Especially in the modern world. It is nearly impossible to tell what is real and what is not. The evolution of the mass media is so far ahead of societies abilities to wrap their collective heads around it, no wonder we have grown so cynical and frustrated. No wonder people become disengaged and remote. There are very few truths left to hang your hat on.

It is not unusual for a young person to relate real life experiences to scenes in movies. Since much of their real life experiences are drawn from some sort of digital media, they conflate reality with video content. They quote movie dialogue, and claim they know some fact because they made a movie about it!

Indeed, the emotional impact of news and fictional events are difficult to separate. The TV coverage of the attack on the World Trade Towers, as shocking as it was, certainly looked a lot like much of the recent movie dramas about earthquakes, Martian invasions or global warming calamities.

Until you saw real people purposely leaping eighty stories, choosing to die instantly upon impact than to be slowly burned to death by the jet-fuel flames.

My son has logged thousands of hours playing video war games. Instead of going fishing, surfing or playing a game of pickup basketball at the local playground, kids today log onto a running war game and blast their way into euphoria digitally. I worry about the high level of visual stimulus, and the desensitization and emotional reconditioning these realistic war games have on his long-term cognitive skills and emotional development.

When our family gets together for the holidays, such as Thanksgiving, Christmas, or for a birthday celebration, we try to engage the group in some sort of activity. It usually ends up being a board game. I have noticed many of the more recent games revolve around some pretty nasty stuff. We played a game called Cards Against Humanity. It features cards that ask a question and then present several phrases (answers). Each player selects one card/phrase and it is the object of the game to select which opposing player would be most likely to have said that specific phrase, as whimsical or nonsensical as it may be.

The responses were unbelievably lurid, profane and provocative. I was embarrassed to listen to the vulgarity in front of my now adult children and their grandmother. The "humor" is not just sophomoric, it is downright perverse and mean-spirited.

I see this kind of humor, the kind that finds it's theme in the deprecation of others, to be reprehensible, but common to the millennial and X-generation. All you have to do is watch the past twenty years of Saturday Night Live, Stephen Colbert, or Bill Maher. Their jokes always come at the expense of someone, some personality trait, political or religious belief, some human tragedy, or social conflict. Classic humor, the kind dispensed by icons like Johnny Carson, Bob Hope or even Ellen DeGeneres that points out human conditions, stereotypes, and familiar life circumstances, is nowhere to be found. It is relegated to history because it reflects old attitudes and is deemed too soft.

Entertainment, it seems, has devolved.

Along with the rapid growth in digital electronics, personal communications, worldwide information systems, social networks and personalized delivery systems, what classifies as entertainment has also expanded and become diluted.

There is so much content available, and we are being bombarded by what there is 24/7. What are kids supposed to do? What is left for them to imagine? To discover through game playing, or from idea sharing? Our children have inherited a world that has boxed them out of so many little moments of enlightenment, so many simple pleasures. There is, as the old saying used to go, little left to the imagination.

Compared to my era, where I spent hours playing with little toys, digging in the dirt, pretending to be something (The Lone Ranger, Daniel Boone), or joining friends to spend hours playing board games, or making up our own games. My folks worried about me because I had what they called "an overheated imagination."

Youngsters today can't use their imaginations. They hardly know what the concept means. They are simply incapable of visualizing something that may not even exist. They associate with other ideas and inventions, movies, social movements, social networks, by trading images, but ask them to visualize a living room with different furniture in it, forget it.

Using the mind to visualize, to imagine, to put yourself in somebody else's shoes helps humans to understand, to become more compassionate, to relate to other societies, cultures and lifestyles. And despite claiming to be the most enlightened and tolerant generation in history, in many ways Millennials' and X-Gens' are just the opposite. If you look at the rapid growth of the Ultimate Fighting Championship (UFC) "sport" it is hard to not see a similarity to ancient Roman events, where Emperors threw Christians to the lions or pitted warriors in fight to the death in chariot races.

In Ancient Rome, it seems, the people were similarly jaded; they were not content to see a sporting match, they needed a "spurting match."

"Here we are now. Entertain us!"

Reinventing Normal

I am getting really tired of hearing terms like fifty is the new thirty. Or, orange is the new black.

Everything to this young generation, is ripe for reinventing. Whether it is the definition of family or the process of raising children. From what we eat, to how we recreate, there is nothing sacred anymore.

Every time I turn around, it is the "new normal," again.

It seems like just last week the Food and Drug Administration was telling us to avoid high cholesterol foods. Stay away from eggs and cheese. Avoid red meat, and do not eat donuts. Now they are saying, oops, eggs are OK. In fact, newer studies show that what you eat has "little or no effect" on your cholesterol readings.

So throw everything in your refrigerator out and start all over, again. Is there a situational comedy on TV that represents the traditional family unit? Nope. *Modern Family* is a conglomeration of every combination of mixed social constructions you can think of. I know, it is all meant to be fun...but isn't the family unit an institution that is the foundation on which civilization and social stability are built? Is it wise to experiment with the lives of children, redesigning the nuclear family unit, reinventing role playing, changing the learning tree into a matrix of disjointed and never before tried templates?

Two and a Half Men, The Big Bang Theory, Mike and Molly, The Simpsons, and virtually all of the TV comedies of the past decade, or more, have trashed everything the TV comedies of the 60's and 70's celebrated. Men, particularly fathers, are typically characterized as irrelevant morons, clumsy and unreliable with stereotypical profiles. They are obsessed with TV sports, beer and guns. They rarely work, or in many cases, simply aren't present. The family unit is often made up of single moms who are overworked, overwhelmed with child raising demands and usually very poor. The kids are portrayed as totally self-sufficient and wily, often the smartest person in the room, but isolated and lonely. In other words, TV land is telling us that it takes all kinds of family structures to deal with the complexities of living in the modern world.

But don't count on dad to offer much help.

The old "pre-enlightenment" series, like *Cosby, or Family Ties* or, God forbid, *Seventh Heaven*, are considered relics of the past, never to be revisited again. In fact, it is nearly impossible to find reruns or any evidence that they ever existed in TV archives. The nuclear family unit such as the Huxtable Family is a myth. The idea that Michael J. Fox actually was a Republican TV star is unfathomable today. And in Seventh Heaven, dad was a minister.

Over the past decade, the only ministers seen on TV are being indicted or disgraced.

Then there is daytime TV. What a wasteland! Most hosts are Jerry Springer wannabes, pitting disturbed, angry, abandoned and disrespected women against their good-for-nothing, self-absorbed, irresponsible womanizing and unemployed "significant" others who have impregnated them and then left. Or, worse yet, they are hosted by some do-gooder doctor who wants to help the viewer by showing them how screwed up other people are!

Look at the recent history of the film industry. When was the last time you saw a movie made with an original script? Seriously, most of the movies coming out of Hollywood are rewrites of previous movies or TV scripts. From *Charlie's Angels*, to *the Adams Family*, from *Batman* to *The Fugitive*, all first appeared on television as a series. Or we can choose to go see Friday the 13th (and seven sequels) or remakes of *Godzilla*, *Star Wars* (1 thru 6), *Mission Impossible* (1 thru 3), *Rocky* (1 thru 5), or *Raiders of the Lost Ark* (1 thru 4), and on and on and on.

In 2016, you will be able to see the new versions of *Kung Fu Panda (3)*, *Batman vs. Superman*, *X-Men*, and *Alice-In-Wonderland*. The moviegoer just can't get enough of superheroes, predictable plots, mediocre acting, redundant drama, and especially, high-tech computer generated big screen action. The driving force in Hollywood is, "if it ain't broke, don't fix it."

I think there is a rational explanation for the appeal of super sophomoric film noir; it must be a response to the evening news that is saturated with blood-soaked trauma from every corner of the world. The reality show of all reality shows, the nightly news, is so horrendous, is it any wonder people just want to escape when they go to a theatre? To want to be immersed in make-believe, in familiar, in comfort, knowing, in the end, the good guys are going to prevail! Because in real life, the good guys are increasingly indistinguishable from the bad guys.

And if you listen to Hollywood, this old stuff repackaged as the new stuff, is the new normal.

Confusing Directions

Social media has a knack for sending mixed messages.

Don't you hate it when a friend sends a confusing and unintelligible text message? When it results in a missed appointment or something significant, I want to scream, "Just call me!"

Listening to celebrities brag about their latest Tweet is depressing. Who cares what you had for breakfast you self-absorbed nitwit? When Michelle Obama posted a tweet with the Twitter hashtag "#BringBackOurGirls!" it dominated the news coverage. But it was simultaneously symbolic of our western impotence.

My first impression was, how does advertising your empathy via Twitter actually help? To me, Twitter is just a giant network to broadcast self-important feelings. It is a digital billboard for patting yourself on the back. "Look at me, I just wanted you to share my compassion!"

Some, who criticized her, were lambasted as jerks because it was presumed the critics didn't care about the kidnapped Nigerian students (presumably because they were black and most were Muslim). It occurred to me that the criticism had more to do with the medium, not so much with the messenger or her message.

The terrorist African group Boko Haram kidnaps and enslaved, married, tortured and murdered nearly 300 young schoolgirls -- a story that occupied a column or two in the newspaper for maybe three or four days. There has never been any follow-up or serious international outrage, as compared to the Paris nightclub shootings.

Yes, news broadcasts expressed outrage. Yes, politicians gave emotional speeches about the inhuman treatment by the terrorists. But the truth is, there was no coalition of world leaders holding hands and declaring all-out war on Boko Haram.

Only an idiot would believe that the kidnapping of hundreds of schoolgirls is anything but a sick, perverted act of hatred. Period. I don't care how you cut it; it is depraved.

Please don't misunderstand me. How we, as a civilized society, react to the heinous crime is a subject for discussion. I hope we can agree on that. My question is, why did *this* incident incite such extreme outrage from women, and so little from major political parties and their mostly male leaders?

Could it be that the use of girls as a tool of terror has hit a nerve? Isn't that exactly the point of terrorism, to hit a nerve, to spark outrage and to put fear into the minds of their opponents? Showing absolutely no respect for human life is not new to the terrorist movement. But isolating, kidnapping, torturing, raping and then selling school-aged girls as slaves is beyond the pale.

Killing hundreds of people with large caliber rifles, plastic explosives, and cutting off the heads of innocent journalists gets lots of TV time and provokes media outrage, but when was the last time you saw the First Lady weigh in with her angst, tweeting *#BringBackOurGirls?*

Boko Haram blames western education as the crime these children were committing. Now they want to use them as trade bait, so are we to believe these maniacs really care at all about the girls? Of course not. They are getting exactly what they want, though. And that is projecting a worldwide image that the western world is helpless.

There have been thousands of extreme inhumane acts of kidnapping, murder, and torture since the era of fundamentalist Islamic Jihad began some time back in the late 70's with the kidnapping and murder of the Israeli Olympic team. Obviously, the world wide web didn't exist during the Palestinian terrorist's attack and murder of the Israeli athletes, so it played out live on Olympic TV coverage. The TV medium was a driving force coalescing world opinion against the tactics of terror, but it also proved to terrorists that using innocents was an effective tool of terror.

During the Bosnian war, thousands of Muslim boys were summarily executed by extremists. They were dragged out of their homes and butchered in front of their families. Whole villages were slaughtered including newborn babies in Afghanistan because they were Coptic Christians! But little or none of those crimes received the publicity that modern day terrorist's atrocities do. Besides, those events were seen as part of a broad civil war. Something that factions with long-held hatreds exacted on each other. Some of the horrific crimes were referred to as ethnic cleansing, as though that made it any less irrational.

In every case, the inhumanity was couched in religious terms, the media proclaimed the violence as hatred and then the news moved on to the next headline.

The tide of terror unleashed on the world by the many factions of Muslim extremism has no shame in killing men, women and children who are non-combatants, innocent civilians, and even clergy. A culture of death permeates extremist fundamentalism like the culture of forgiveness permeates the Judeo-Christian ethic.

Boko Haram is simply a bunch of demented narcissists who use a warped stone-age interpretation of the world's largest religion as a justification for their nihilism. Their acts of mayhem feed their compulsion to grab attention, show their anger and disrespect, to dispense sadism, pain and suffering as well as control every aspect of our lives, up to and until they end their pathetic existence on this earth -- the earth they consider corrupted because they can't have their way.

Maybe the problem with Michelle Obama's Twitter plea is that some people see Twitter as a singularly self-obsessed indulgence. When it suddenly becomes a medium of activism, it may someday be effective, but it will have to wade through a ton of irrelevant blather before it reaches serious proportions. The critics are simply suggesting that maybe we should use something a little more 'serious' to project our outrage and to actuate change.

The message *#BringBackOurGirls* begs the question; how? It trivializes the effort that will be required to actually accomplish such a feat.

When the First Lady is using Twitter to scream online "someone please help us!" it sounds a little desperate. She is, after all, the better half of the most powerful man on the planet, right?

Beware of Men

Our First Lady could be working on something closer to home that we can actually accomplish. Like "bringing back our men". Seriously, America has a problem. Though our country is full of males, there is a growing shortage of "Men."

By that I mean, the traditional role that men have played in society has atrophied. And I believe it is the result of a series of cultural trends that have formed a perfect storm, a torrential rain of cultural decisions denying men their historically respected role as leader of the family. The world is experiencing a profound realignment of the traditional role of the sexes. Lead by the women's liberation movement, men increasingly find themselves in a gray area of irrelevance. This is not to say that we should, or could, ever go back to the place in history where men truly walked all over women. It is just an attempt to put into perspective some of the astonishing events that are occurring at an increasingly alarming rate: I am speaking about two sides of the same coin.

Why are we seeing so many seemingly unexplainable mass murders involving young men slaughtering innocent people, mostly other young people or school children? Why is there a growing movement of young Muslim men anxiously volunteering to blow themselves up while simultaneously slaughtering other innocent Muslims (and Christians and Jews) while screaming 'God is Great!"?

What is the common denominator between young extremist Islamic terrorists committing murder-suicide of innocent people and young middle=class privileged American males using high powered military style weapons to commit murder-suicide of innocent bystanders? Their disease has near identical symptoms because the underlying chemistry in the cultural petri dish is the same. They are acting out their anger, loneliness, sexual and psychological disorientation and alienation from all norms of society.

Why is this pandemic cultural disease affecting only men? Let's look at the state of men in our society.

- Disproportionately high unemployment
- High rates of family dysfunction and divorce, depression, PTSD
- Gender confusion
- Hostility towards women
- Decreasing graduation rates
- Inability to form long term relationships
- Loss of trust and empathy for others
- Lack of anger control
- Sexual deviancy and high incarceration rates
- Increasing gang influence
- Self-destructive behavior and lack of remorse
- Mass murder of children and students

This is a huge problem. The statistics are overwhelming, that men and boys are suffering from all of these maladies at astonishingly high rates, with the volume and severity of them metastasized right about the time the women's rights movement began in the early '60s. The numbers have grown exponentially since then, both in Western and Islamic culture. Probably not a causative relationship, but certainly a contributing one.

Yes, I believe the modern day terrorist is in an indirect way, a product of many of the same forces that are influencing young males in the West. In fact, the FBI has said, more and more young American men are attracted to and actively joining Jihad. And thought the cultural atmospheres are diametrically opposed, both the eastern culture and the western culture have seen enormous changes as they relate to the male species in the past fifty years.

Internationally, Islamic fundamentalist extremists display nearly identical profiles of American mass murderers. Have you ever noticed that young Islamic males are abandoned to their mothers by the Islamic code assigning all child raising duties to the enslaved women so the men can attend religious functions, tribal assemblies and to focus solely on themselves? Islamic fundamentalist men use their religion as an excuse, but the results are very much the same. Fundamentalist Muslim fathers take no responsibility for their children. Their women basically raise the children alone and must be the male role model for their sons.

Moderate Muslims rationalize extremist violence by blaming extreme poverty, disrespect for Muslim values, anger at western displays of pornography, extreme wealth, abuse of alcohol, drugs and blasphemy of Allah.

In the western culture, we have over five decades of marginalization of marriage and the family unit, organized religion, and the rejection of authority. Everything has been focused on the preservation of youth, and the abandonment of any form of self-denial and social or sexual accountability.

The inner city dynamics mimic that of the Muslims; fatherless households, women assuming the child rearing duties, suffering economic hardship, and the young, alienated males migrating towards nihilism, and gang affiliations.

The explosion of mass murders has been perpetrated by angry males, who are typically disenfranchised, emotionally disfigured and abandoned, convinced that the whole world is against them, confused by the denial of traditional male entitlement, and driven by extreme narcissism. They act out by taking on the role of a malevolent God, and viciously terminating the lives of the children of the women who have stolen their manhood. They manufacture all kinds of rationales, but to these sick people, their abuse of power is sweet revenge!

These violent humans are the extreme, obviously. But they are the proverbial canary in the coal mine of civilization. And they are not "men" by any definition. They are acting more like abused animals.

If you separate a puppy from its mother at a young age, use force to discipline it, keep it locked up as it grows rapidly, don't allow it to socialize, give it no love and attention, keep it in a constant state of insecurity and agitation, and reward it for aggressive behavior, you get a dangerous wild animal that will explode in violence at the slightest threat.

Sound familiar?

Men are a lot like dogs: they tend to be task oriented, respond well to affection and affirmation. Men understand and thrive in hierarchies, they feel most comfortable when they know their role and can respond to expectations. Men are problem solvers by nature and will become frustrated when they are stymied by cultural counter forces. When a dog is given attention, understandable, compassionate and deliberate discipline, they respond with unconditional love to their masters.

Likewise, men who assume the lead of the family, who accept the implied responsibility of providing sustenance and security to their family, typically thrive.

The opposite of that is the phenomenon of social aggression, whether in the form of gangs, criminal organizations or even military forces. Men naturally form hierarchies and alliances to maintain an element of control. The growth of the gang culture is demonstratively a result of the lack of father figures, especially in the inner city culture. Ask any gangster what the appeal is, and he will inevitably say, "my homies are like family to me."

Here are some of the ways young men are characterized in modern progressive culture:

- Dismissed as untrustworthy philanderers
- Responsible for war, hunter killers
- Domineering and disrespectful of women, sexist
- Selfish and discriminatory, racist
- Clumsy, careless and foolish
- Historically benefit from white preferential treatment

Starting with the Sexual Revolution of the 1960's, virtually all institutions of learning have taught a doctrine of female-centric, male bashing curriculum reflecting the belief that men have caused most of the world's problems, and it will be women who will eventually deliver us from self-destruction.

Fifty years later, men are disproportionately underemployed. They are entering and graduating from college at dramatically lower rates than women. The marriage rate is way down, as is the birth rate. Young men are living with their parents to an average age of 27. Boys are far more likely to end up in the juvenile justice system, and men in prison than women are. In every category of causes of premature death, men and boys suffer much higher rates than women and girls. Men are having serious problems emotionally and especially romantically. In fact, it is hard to find men who truly understand intimacy anymore. Just ask the girls.

We can argue about the divorce rate, but the truth is, the person who suffers the most from divorce is the son(s). They are often subjected to harsh trials where the father is characterized as the demon because obviously a lot of money is at stake and the women must do that to protect her financial status. Custody and visitation are typically skewed toward the mother, so a boy-of-divorce sees much less of his dad, and the influence he would have to be a role model is greatly reduced. The son often blames himself and then develops feelings of abandonment and extreme resentment, even hatred of his mom, while secretly looking for ways to validate his manhood, to prove to his unengaged father that he has value and can act independently, especially to an extreme degree.

The resulting conflict, the confusion about the alienation of everyone he loves, the pressure to not be the chauvinistic male his hormones are telling him to be, engenders itself in thoughts of suicide, revenge and self-hatred.

Do the math; if over 50% of marriages end in divorce in America, as some analysis would indicate, what does that do to our ability as a society to raise boys who can then become good fathers? The argument that marriage is a failed institution is a slippery slope and rapidly becoming a self-fulfilling prophecy. But is the high rate of divorce necessarily a result of the nature of the institution, or has it been seriously damaged by the explosion of female egocentrism the past half century?

Men and especially boys have become so increasingly irrelevant and their existence marginalized, that many have adopted a more feminized profile, wearing gender neutral clothes, hairstyles, and jewelry. Shaving facial and body hair, and even speaking in feminine narratives. For many men, hooking up with another male is not purely a sexual predilection, it is just easier.

All of this is to say that the proverbial writing is on the wall; we just need to recognize it and also accept that we are the reason this wave of male dysfunction is cresting. Baby boomers have selfishly focused too much on their own lives, refused to grow up and to accept adult responsibility, and the need for self-sacrifice required to properly nurture, teach and demonstrate what a parent, not just a friend, should be. We need to understand and accept the natural role of the male species in the physical, physiological and emotional lifespan of the human being.

We have forgotten to take care of our boys. The result: A generation of males that don't know how to be men.

CHAPTER THREE

Caution: School Zone

" The problem isn't that Johnny can't read.
The problem isn't that Johnny can't think.
The problem is that Johnny doesn't know what thinking is;
he confuses it with feeling."

— Thomas Sowell

Turn Signals

"It depends on what the meaning of 'is' is."

—President William Jefferson Clinton,
testifying before a Grand Jury in 1998

Education is a word that is hard to define. It is an even more mysterious and illusive concept. In fact, it should go down in history as the most misunderstood, misquoted and misused word or concept in the vocabulary of public policy. Politicians want to give it away to buy votes, parents shop it around looking for the best deals on brand names like Harvard, Notre Dame and Penn State, so they can give their kids an advantage; employers demand it, but won't necessarily pay for it, and students still can't tell you what it meBut education is not a commodity. It is not something you can bestow on someone.

Education describes a state of being that is accumulated over years of hard work and study. The most insincere promise any politician can make is to suggest that their policies can give our children a great education. Unless or until a person commits to a long period of intense immersion in understanding complex information, they cannot simply acquire an education.

My personal college experience was mostly esoteric. I spent most of my four years in a California State University writing meaningless essays, collaborating on useless projects, and participating in long-winded lecture hall debates, and partying.

I got out of college what I put into college, pretty much nothing. The sad fact is I did little serious study while spending my parents hard earned money. But the point is, the majority of young people aren't mature enough to recognize the importance of the moment and how much they will regret not taking every advantage available to them while they are attending college. So it is up to the instructors, the professors and the administration to summon their interest, to arouse their intellect, and to push them when necessary, to bear down and learn something.

Some of my instructors were successful with me, but most were not.

When I was in college, the Vietnam War was still raging. In fact, I received a draft deferment for four years, just before the lottery was instituted, so I was lucky to avoid conscription.

Our war-divided nation experienced painful losses, both in young human inventory but also in cultural identity and confidence. In what I have always thought is an incredible irony, many of the social conflicts of the 60's and 70's was not much different than today; campus unrest was driven by the unjust and racist war, civil rights and white privilege, the sexual revolution (women's equality, abortion and male hegemony), the widespread use of marijuana, the role of religion in western society, and the redistribution of wealth. Much of my time on campus was devoted to rallies, speeches or concerts on the grass. The early seventies were the very beginning of the infiltration of post cold war leftism.

The point is, just like the college experience today, students can get great knowledge from their instruction and collaborations in college, or they can waste some very good educational opportunities and end up accomplishing very little in the way of gaining marketable skills.

Which path a student follows is entirely up to them.

But one thing remains embedded in the modern college experience; indoctrination. The time that our children spend in schools, under the care of teaching professionals, has continued to increase. Whether it is elementary school followed by afternoon extension classes or paid child care, or high school and extracurricular activities, all the way into and through college, our kids are subjected to training by others for the majority of their early lives. The values and information taught to them during these enormous periods of time will have an influence on their impressionable minds for years, or even generations to come.

For most people it is easy to trust these educational/child care professionals implicitly. We walk away in the morning or at the curb or airport as we wave goodbye and hope they are in good hands. But if some of the most recent events concerning the anger and disillusionment, the sense of alienation students across the country feel, is any indication, many of the educational elite's definition of "good hands" is not necessarily the same as yours and mine.

Missing the Onramp

A series of National studies have shown that our schools are turning out students unprepared for the real world. I remember talking to a UPS delivery man as he checked off the packages using a digital scanner. They move so fast, and when he told me his workload I was astonished. How can you possibly deliver that many packages in one day, I asked?

It would not be possible without technology. "Back in the day," he said, "we only used paper receipts and stickers to keep track of the packages. It was hard and slow. But in our modern business, we have a myriad of other problems."

Like what, I asked. "We can't find enough good employees."

He went on to tell me that big companies like UPS have to do extensive retraining before they can put someone out in a truck. And even then, he says, it is hard because "so many young people simply have no work ethic, seem to think they shouldn't have to answer to anyone and can't solve problems on their own."

"They can't handle the supervision, can't fit in, so they work for a few months and quit."

I had an interesting, and I think revealing discussion with a friend of mine who teaches college level ethics. In a recent classroom debate, one team was assigned to defend "traditional marriage", and the other to defend "going it alone".

The debate assignment was, "Is it worth getting married?"

She said she loved the way the students came prepared. They would lay out their cases, with both teams doing a great job of describing the good and bad aspects of marriage. It was raucous and energetic, and a lot of fun. The students seemed to enjoy the clash of ideas.
"What did they decide?" I asked.

"They didn't," she said. "That was not the objective. That would have been too judgmental. It was just an exercise!"

I was shocked. Like anything in life, marriage is not for everyone. But it makes no sense to me for young college-age students to be discussing the moral equivalency of forgoing marriage over the hard work and total commitment it takes to make a lifelong commitment to a spouse, and the children that may result from that union.

The nuclear family, it seems, is a thing of the past as far as our public school system is concerned. And the modern day birth rate, which is plunging, is a frightening indicator that the future of a strong traditional family structure is in deep doo doo.

This moral vacuum is demonstrated in many ways, but the traditional core family unit seems to be a regular target. Considered by the left to be just another construct of male misogyny to enslave women, our kids are being taught that any form of a family unit is no less equal than any other. Parents are characterized as controlling and judgmental, and by default promoting an unenlightened view of family, community and personal freedom.

"Any parent," writes professor William Kilpatrick, "who has traditional ideas about right and wrong (in a classroom discussion) is likely to suffer by comparison."

Teachers, in classroom groups, will often tell students, "Your parents don't understand you, but we do."

Studies that elevate student self-esteem, he notes, are quite popular with the students, since they focus on their favorite subject, themselves. And it reinforces their predilection for independence from their parents.

A National Commission On Excellence in Education Report, titled *A Nation at Risk* was published in 1983. It was prescient in its scathing assessment of what our kids are doing while they are in class.

> "...secondary school curricula have been homogenized, diluted, and diffused to the point that they no longer have a central purpose. In effect, we have a cafeteria-style curriculum in which the appetizers and the desserts can easily be mistaken for the main course."

That characterization has only gotten worse, with a proliferation of social studies classes about homosexuality, transgender identity issues, workplace discrimination, environmental destruction and racial diversity classes dominating the curricula.

Students must be concerned, just as most modern employees are, with workplace issues like discrimination, hate speech, sexual harassment or innuendo, and many other potentially dangerous politically charged situations that could lead to suspensions, or even lawsuits. Most of these rules were ignited by the NEA or student unions, and they just keep piling up.

School campuses are incubators for every imaginable crusade on earth: global warming, women's rights and abortion, food additives and animal rights, children's vaccination scares, discrimination issues about language, looks, weight, sports, and any conceivable minority or small group or lineage students and their teachers can find.

Colleges routinely hold conferences and seminars to identify new causes to support, always contrary to normal status quo, because, I presume, to support the status quo would not be learning. Along the way, many of these divisive issues attract corporate dollars in the form of subsidies, grants and advertising. Some of the issues work their way into mainstream curriculum, as "environmental studies" or "black history." They ultimately become vehicles for ideological indoctrination.

It is not so much the political slant that is alarming as it is just a huge waste of time and resources that could go to more pertinent and productive studies and programs.

Increasing Federal and State government regulations cost millions of precious education funds to conform to stupid laws about where to place fire extinguishers, the color of textbooks, the paint on bathroom walls, who can treat students with a stomach ache, and exactly what can and cannot be done about it. Union rules determine or control admissions, athletic programs, student publications, food distribution and preparations, menus, bathroom access, even what deodorant or cologne can be worn in class.

As with everything in the western world, money plays a big part of the problem with our schools. It is the money that the unions are addicted to, and that school administrators must keep flowing. In addition to the growth of the teaching bureaucracy and the commensurate costs, outside commercial interests are invading the classroom, and a disturbing picture is beginning to crystallize. So much money is flying around the school environment, but less and less of it is actually being used to teach our kids real world skills.

At the University of Maryland, Northrop-Grumman Corporation is designing and helping build a new dormitory, paying for computers and supplies in the cybersecurity department, and helping format the program curricula because the school is short of funds.

The Wall Street Journal, in a piece published last year, said:

> "International Business Machines Corp. deepened a partnership with Ohio State University to train students in big-data analytics. Murray State University in Kentucky recently retooled part of its engineering program, with financial support and guidance from local companies. And the State University of New York College of Nanoscale Science and Engineering in Albany and other locations is expanding its footprint after attracting billions of dollars of private-sector investments."

Though these partnerships have been around at the graduate level and among the nation's polytechnic schools and community colleges, they are now migrating into traditional undergraduate programs.

The emerging model is a "new form of the university," said Wallace Loh, president of the University of Maryland. "What we are seeing is a federal grant university that is increasingly corporate and increasingly reliant on private philanthropy."

As budgets stretch, funds become less available for curricula development, so corporations are compelled to step in if they want to find ready-to-work employees. Many larger engineering companies have done their own studies because they have not been able to find students properly prepared for their industry.

In that same study the Wall Street Journal points out:

> "The result: about 30% of recent college graduates with bachelor's degrees have jobs that are better suited to those with high-school diplomas or associate's degrees, according to the Center on Education and the Workforce at Georgetown University."

At the same time, a recent Gallup poll found that only 11% of business leaders strongly agree that college graduates have the necessary skills and competencies to succeed in the workplace. This would explain the motives of business to put financial and human resources to work on college campuses. They need to influence the direction of study if they ever want to find students who can help them.

But isn't that to be expected when it is obvious our schools are too busy indoctrinating kids instead of actually preparing them for work in the real world? The evidence is clear that most 4-year college students spend the majority of their time on meaningless social studies, and little time really understanding serious science, business, or finance.

In a yearbook called *Feeling, Valuing and the Art of Growing*, published by the Association of Supervision and Curriculum Development as a guide to student "growth" agendas, it states:

> "Literacy is not good enough. More is needed to live a personally satisfying life. (Students must be educated in)...perceiving from any and varied perspectives; communicating thoughts and feelings in reciprocally honest and constructive ways...
> We believe that for maximum richness of living, each person must be valued for himself, with his uniqueness, recognized and not only respected, but revered."

The common high school or college campus resembles the workplace more than a place to study and learn. It has all of the trappings of a major manufacturing plant where the main concern is the health and welfare of the workers, and their cash generating productivity, as opposed to the traditional idea of a campus where students feel unencumbered by the worries of everyday existence so they can focus their energies on debate, discussion, reading and lectures.

Not only are major college sports programs (i.e., football) huge money makers, they reflect the corporate attitude about cash streams that preoccupy college and high school administrations across the country.

You could say that academia, and specifically the income-oriented departments like sports, are the most narcissistic of all.

Roadside Services

Remember Monica Lewinsky, the White House intern that became the center of a worldwide firestorm over her tryst with President Bill Clinton? She is now touring and selling her book about how she was victimized by the political class, the women rights advocates, the news media and just about everyone she can think of. It would be easy to feel sorry for her because she certainly was victimized. Not just by the President, but long before that by her misguided upbringing. She was the child of a bra-burning, feminist mother who did not practice monogamy (might explain Monica's total lack of concern for Hillary, the spouse), an over-achieving workaholic father who had little time for little Monica (might explain her need for love from powerful men), and her still to this day reluctance to show any remorse or guilt about participating in a scandal that nearly brought about the removal from office of a sitting President (explained by her as "passions and commitments" and books and tours congratulating herself for surviving the media victimhood she describes as "suffocating").

So the bottom line is, we have been so successful at training our children through the channels of advanced education, that we see an overwhelming number of celebrities and well "educated" professionals celebrating their victimhood, disdaining or at least trivializing, the institution of marriage, promoting promiscuity as a virtue, congratulating themselves for immoral behavior, and flaunting their psycho-science of environmentalism, Scientology and numerous other wacky experimental and self-serving religions.

Monica is the perfect spokesperson for self-indulgence, denial and youthful rejection of all things that ever went before her.

If her experience is any indication there is a serious and disturbing trend toward self-idolatry, I believe this is tied to the concept of humanism. We Americans have always rejected the institutionalization of any religion in our schools, and I agree wholeheartedly with that idea. But we must also be diligent that a curriculum that defines itself as non-religious may not be what we typically refer to as religious, yet may have similar traits and impacts.

Make no mistake about it, people who call themselves humanist, are indeed religious. Religion is by definition a belief system. If we are not careful, if we allow the institutions of academia to get away with it; humanism will become a state-sanctioned religion disguised as a socially sensitive learning curricula.

By making the practice of humanism, the veneration of the individual, and elevating the earth to the status of mother of all that lives, the default belief system of institutionalized education, our kids are being indoctrinated, pure and simple.

From those who screamed the loudest protesting Christmas decorations and music, who complained about God being on our coins or in our Pledge of Allegiance or National Anthem, that they were having someone else's morals and convictions shoved down their throats, if we don't wake up and pay attention, we will end up having theirs shoved down ours.

The Toll Road

There is a monetary incentive driving the national educational establishment to perpetuate its dogma and to control the local educational agenda. If you or I should bring this up at a cocktail party or a school board meeting, we will be shouted down by a chorus of defenders who will repeat the mantra that public schools are underfunded.

They will say it is shameful that professional athletes make millions while teachers are at the lowest end of the pay scale.

Parents are made to feel guilty that schools are falling apart, the air-conditioning doesn't work, the roof leaks, and there are never enough computers to go around. The implication is that the parents have been too interested in their own retirement investments to properly fund public education.

If we would submit to a small tax increase, at least we could make the schools safe. That we will never attract great teachers if we continue to offer less than a living wage. Minorities face adverse conditions from poor teachers to lousy school conditions, so they start life at a disadvantage. That if we offered all minorities a free education we could reduce crime and homelessness, poverty and the destruction of the family unit.

When conservatives suggest setting aside some money to promote charter schools, or that allowing workers to fund their own children's education through a voucher system, would give students and their parents more skin in the game. The educational elites complain that diverting any public money to support private schools of any kind would destroy the public school system altogether.

And since it is working so well, why rock the boat?

Recent studies indicate that nearly $10,000 is spent, per student, per year, in California's public school system. Though the trail of where the money actually goes is obscured by tricky education bureaucrat's complicated budgeting processes, it isn't hard to assume that much of the money is being used for management, maintenance, asset acquisition, and hundreds of other non-classroom applications.

A Brookings Institute study concluded, "when other relevant factors are taken into account, economic resources are unrelated to student achievement."

Besides, the per day revenue figures just don't add up. If a student costs $10,000 a year, and class size averages 25, that's $250,000 a year toward a classroom. Subtract the annual salary of the teacher, plus an additional 20% for all other administrative positions (i.e., $120,000.00), and you have $130K left to spend on that child. Enough to pay for all the classroom supplies, the books and computers, field trips, art supplies, and maybe even a limousine to drive the student to and from class every day!

A study in New York found that only about two-thirds of their annual per student revenues actually reached the classroom, the other one-third was deflected to other administrative accounts. I think it's fair to assume those percentages apply generically.

But studies show that math and science scores are way down. While class sizes are up by 20%, (which intuitively suggests more per class cash) college teacher populations are also up 20%.

And though we spend a great deal more per student than many other industrialized nations, our results are much worse. America is currently ranked 12th for science and math. Since 1952, our SAT verbal scores have dropped over 54%!

Meanwhile, college tuitions have skyrocketed. Since private college tuition can be the second or third largest financial outlay most people ever have (behind only a home mortgage or remodeling your house) it only makes sense that a parent would want to be sure their student will be well prepared for adulthood upon graduation.

The Economic Institute released a study recently, about the plight of young college and high school grads with respect to the job market. In what I view as an indictment of the blind spot so much of our college-educated think-tank intellectuals have to the realities of free market capitalism, they espouse the same wrong-headed progressive-socialism that has put this country into the cultural pothole we find ourselves in today.

Their conclusions are we need more of the same. We need more government regulation, more financial and tax policy coercion to force employers to hire more people they don't need, and to pay them for non-productive leaves, and to increase the minimum wage to pay more for less.

The rising cost of college combined with the failure of wages to grow for young college graduates signals that a college education is becoming a more uncertain investment. The college premium, or the relative edge young workers receive in earnings from obtaining a college degree, experienced rapid growth in the 1980s and 1990s, but the growth has been relatively slow since 2000. Any rise in the premium that has occurred in the last 15 years is due to larger wage losses for high school graduates, rather than strong wage growth for college graduates...

The bottom line is that for recent college graduates, finding a good job has become much more difficult. These findings are consistent with other research showing that among the workforce as a whole, there has been a decline in the demand for "cognitive skills" since 2000.

In order to create full employment, the Federal Reserve Board must prioritize low rates of unemployment when making monetary policy and not raise interest rates, which would prematurely slow the economy. Greater public investment would also help; Congress can enact targeted employment programs and direct funds to infrastructure improvements to create jobs. (Public-sector employment is still down half a million jobs since the Great Recession began, without even accounting for population growth.) In order to spur wage growth, we must pursue <u>policies that strengthen workers' collective bargaining rights, as well as update and strongly enforce labor standards.</u> In particular, we should raise the minimum

wage, update the overtime threshold, provide earned sick leave
and paid family leave, regularize undocumented workers, and end
discriminatory practices that contribute to race and gender inequities.

From; The Class of 2015: Despite an Improving Economy, Young
Grads Still Face an Uphill Climb
By Elise Gould Ph.D., Economics, University of Wisconsin at
Madison
Alyssa Davis, B.A. The University of Texas at Austin
Will Kimball, B.A., Economics and Political Science, University
of Connecticut}

The Economic Institute think tank employees were, without exception, trained by some of our best professors! They have been indoctrinated to believe that government is the answer to all of our cultural anomalies. They have become efficient at interpreting data to get the results they want.

They are good comrades in the march towards socializing America.

When reading their report, it becomes apparent that the impact of the terrorist attacks on the World Trade Center in 2001, or the ongoing series of wars and civil disruption worldwide, isn't even a factor in their thesis. In their own words, they consider the Great Recession the main problem, without for a moment considering why that recession was so great. Or why banks were making highly risky home mortgage loans to people who couldn't pay them back.

Did it ever come into their minds that the destruction to the worldwide bank portfolios that came from the interruption in banking operations for nearly six months after 911 might have had something to do with the risk/reward policies of major investment groups? Or that Congress, in its zeal to "level the playing field" for minorities to gain home ownership, had rescinded laws that reduced bank exposure to uncollectible loans? That the humongous interjection of government aid to bail out the plunderers of Wall Street might just have had the opposite effect?

That the artificial low-interest rate (no interest rate) lending standards imposed by the Fed have encouraged unrestrained federal spending, pushing our national debt past twenty trillion dollars?

That the combined punitive corporate tax policies and onerous employee rights protections, benefits and costs of insurance of the past half century might explain the flight of manufacturing jobs? Did it ever occur to them that the high cost of health care may just be a by-product of onerous liability insurance costs?

Apparently not.

It did not occur to them that tort reform might go a long way to reduce all of the above because they have no idea how much non-essential, victim compensation driven litigation is costing our economy.

It didn't occur to them because that would go against everything they have been taught to know and understand about the national economy. About how, when given the chance, spreadsheet know-it-all pinheads in the various departments (of commerce, of trade, of finance and education and employment and resources and state and on and on) will, using all of their advanced degrees in civil service and government bureaucracies, try to legislate and regulate our way to full employment and prosperity.

Instead, they recommend "greater public investment" (taxes), more government hiring, increased collective bargaining rights, that we raise the minimum wage, increase overtime, sick and family leave compensation, and to push for more regulation of race and gender inequality litigation!

They have been taught the socialist handbook for complete free market financial collapse. Pretty close to what we have right now after nearly fifty years of our educational system being hijacked by barely disguised Marxist professors and two terms of Obama's top-down economic mismanagement.

The academic elites are not the only ones with gunpowder burns. They are actually benefactors of a much larger, and more dangerous beast: Unions and Union collaborations.

The National Education Association teacher's union is the largest organized employee's union in the world, followed not too far behind by the American Federation of Teachers, as the sixth largest union. They wield enormous power over many levels of government, of financial markets, and of political parties too. Besides the growing number of teachers and educational administrators nationwide, unions have invaded just about every level of government. Whether it is ambulance drivers or airport traffic controllers, unions hold sway over working conditions, wages and benefits, pensions and just about every bodily function that is addressed in their contracts.

Did you know that 49% of all US union workers are government employees?

In the educational employment environment, unions dictate the rules of engagement. College professors can't be fired because they have tenure. Recent cases have demonstrated that even when accused of sexual assault, it is virtually impossible to fire them. They may be suspended, but even then it is usually with pay. The time and effort it takes to investigate charges discourages most officials from making a serious effort to dismiss even the worst offenders.

The unions dictate everything from administrator's hours and conditions to the number of hours' students "must" attend class. The combined forces of the NEA (National Education Association) and AFT (Associated Federation of Teachers) is the single largest contributor to state and federal election campaigns. Much of their cash comes from money they take from members, in some cases without the member's approval. Recent court rulings continue to allow those unions to confiscate "donations" from worker paychecks, which can then be given to candidates who comply with union demands.

One of America's premier critics of Big Education is Thomas Sowell. He said:

"There has been a progressively more politicized, esoteric, and self-indulgent set of tendencies in Academia...these symbolize the new scholasticism, with its inbred self-congratulatory nihilism and its abdication of traditional responsibilities of training the young... and the strength of the Union will insure the continuation of the lifestyles the bureaucracy enjoys."

When I went to college in the early seventies, I can remember the system was like the old saying Russian dissidents used to describe their economic lot in life: "We pretend to work, and they pretend to pay us." In our US school systems, students pretended to actually learn something while teachers pretended to actually teach something.
I saw a quote from a well-known and respected critic of the American educational system. Chester E. Finn who said, "American education is to education what the Soviet economy is to economy."

It is a sham, an illusion. Certainly there are ways to get something out of it, but it isn't the well-oiled machine the state would have you believe it is.

In a study written by Finn and Diane Ravitch called *What Do Our Seventeen Year Olds Know?* they discovered that:

- 43% of high school students couldn't place World War II between 1900 and 1950.
- 75% were unable to say within 20 years when Lincoln was President
- Only 2 of 3 knew the Declaration of Independence marked the colonists break with England's tyranny

In his book, *The De-Valuing of America*, author Bill Bennett states that his experience as a former Secretary of Education, whenever parents were asked what they wanted from their schools, "they consistently put two tasks at the top of their list: first, teach our children how to speak, write, read, think and count correctly. Second, help them to develop reliable standards of right and wrong that will guide them through life."

He goes on to note, however, when at an educational conference he stated this view, he was roundly criticized by four State Commissioners of Education. They had their preferred missions: "To help students cope with life: to increase global awareness and to change the shape and focus of America".

Doesn't it seem contradictory that what parents want their kids to learn is in direct conflict with what academia wants to teach?

The clash of these two distinctly divergent views of the role of education and religion in society is precisely reflective of the cultural war we are currently embroiled in. In the micro world, the battle rages over student sensitivities, while in the macro world, Islamic Jihadists demand we accept their version of Islam and Sharia Law.

In the micro world of academia, battles rage over bilingual studies and the view that native languages should be preserved and that the idea that there should be a default national language is racist and intolerant. Classes that study African heritage, women's suffering, or animal rights, serve to divide students, to create cultural frictions and to turn impressionable minds away from traditions and cultural icons of the image of America, as the land of the free.

As our people become increasingly sensitive to innumerable distinctions of race, heritage, social class, color of eyes or sexual practices, we have become a country less willing to form judgments. The standard of a whole new generation of value-neutral youth is "Who am I to judge?"

Armed with all kinds of newly collected data, reams of studies and years of politically corrected history, our educationally well-endowed students refuse to apply their own critical thinking because it would contradict their moral ambivalence.

The institutionalized opposition to traditional curricula can be traced to the early seventies, which parallels my college experience. "Values Clarification" became the mantra of the educational elite, wherein children were encouraged to determine their own values, because the Christian values typically incorporated in schools by the 10 Commandments were deemed an unacceptable ideological form of judgmental and racist coercion.

In hindsight, it was the earliest attempts to destroy the Judeo-Christian ethic so indigenous to the American Way.

It was the genesis of what is today the prominent "Moral Relativism" movement that has bastardized our school system. In an article published in the New York Times, a college professor asked his students what they would do if they found $1000 in an abandoned or lost purse. The professor suggested that he could not advise the students because, "If I come from a position of what is right and what is wrong, then I am not their counselor."

That should be a turn signal. It should elicit outrage from parents, but it has not. In fact, it comports with the parenting trend of letting kids make up their own minds, make all of their own decisions, regardless of the consequences. Many parents have simply abdicated their roles in order to avoid conflict.

A survey conducted among college students across several well-respected campuses found that when confronted with a moral dilemma, nearly 80% refused to make an ethical judgment, reasoning that there was no "black or white" answer, especially if the question had a moral aspect to it.

When I get into a discussion about ethics and morals, if we can avoid the "left vs. right" debate altogether, it still comes down to the issue of morals evolving around some "religious" connotation. By attaching the culturally explosive buzz word "religion" to the concept of morality, the academics have "liberated" themselves from any sort of responsibility to define or expose "truths" or "judgments" of any consequence.

If the tenants of a church or belief system are in parallel and support the basic ideals of a good education, then what is so threatening about posting the 10 Commandments on a wall, or allowing those who wish to have a moment of silence for prayer, just before the start of class?

If the long-held traditions and practices of any religion or "life management system" proves to be effective in producing happy, peace loving, well-adjusted and community centered citizens, who cares where it came from?

Marxists do. It matters to them because any form of religion other than worship of the nanny state is a threat to complete control of the individual and the populace. Am I suggesting that anyone who objects to making the tenants of the 10 commandments part of our school curricula must be a Marxist? The answer is yes, whether it is a conscious reflection of their thinking or just a subtle part of their passivity and indifference.

Unfortunately, in the halls of academia, Christianity is considered a superstition and dismissed along the lines of a baseball player's fear that by washing his lucky shirt, he may cause the team to lose the big game.

It is also viewed as an existential threat. Just recently a High School Principal decided that Santa Claus, Thanksgiving and the Pledge of Allegiance are just too "white" and threatening to minorities and non-believers, so she banned any symbols of them.

In another incident, kindergarten students in a New York public school were coached to create a mock International flag, by layering cut up canvas and using colored pencils and crayons, they represented 22 other nations. They stitched them together and totally defaced a series of American flags, then at the bottom they wrote: "We pledge allegiance to an International Flag."

Just to outrage the public even more, the local PTA auctioned the flags off as a fundraiser, for themselves!

Their attitude of self-importance and misinformed certitude is offensive. This is just another example of college indoctrinated teachers who have been made functionally illiterate by academic political correctness and left-wing socialist workers ideology gone wild.

CHAPTER FOUR

Following Directions

"Over the years, the United States has sent many of its fine
young men and women
into great peril to fight for freedom beyond our borders.
The only amount of land we have ever asked for in return
is enough to bury those that did not return."

— Colin Powell

Promises

Before you read another page in this book, I would ask you to indulge me, and stand and repeat The Pledge of Allegiance:

"I pledge allegiance
to the flag
of the United States of America,
and to the Republic,
for which it stands
indivisible, under God, with liberty and justice for all."

Now, please take a few seconds to think about what you just did. Think about the feelings you have right now, and especially the feelings you may have when you are asked to repeat this in a public setting.

Did you really mean what you just said? Or was it something you did out of a sense of obligation? Or did you say it because of a sense of shame you may have if you did not? Or did you ask yourself, "I wish I felt that way, but I don't?"

Ask yourself:

- Why do you know this pledge and when did you learn it?
- Do you recall ever feeling weird about repeating it?
- Have you ever questioned its basic tenets?
- Are you OK with the "Under God" part?
- What exactly does the word "allegiance" mean?

OK, thank you for going along with me on this little journey.

Now that I have planted some questions in your mind, and perhaps rattled your cage just a little bit, I want to explain myself. I am a 60's generation, baby boomer. I spent my formative years challenging authority, resisting the draft, defining the sexual revolution, and losing my inhibitions to drugs. There was a time when I liked to get naked and streak public events.

I was a Beatles fan, a music fan, a hippie, a student protester, and an extreme libertine. I was a part of a movement. Something I was initially very proud of. I was, in my mind, looking at the world from a new perspective, and taking it to Nirvana.

John Lennon's "Imagine" became my personal, national anthem. I liked the idea that we should all live in peace without borders. He suggested we take religion out of our vocabulary. But in most schools in America today, children no longer recite the Pledge of Allegiance, or if they do, any student who objects for any reason is allowed to sit it out.

The message is, The Pledge is no longer an essential element of growing up in America. In fact, on average, most schools and public events have stopped using it at all. Many liberals look at The Pledge as a symbol of American imperialism and xenophobia, and it imparts a militaristic and aggressively nationalistic arrogance in children.

I want to try to put the Pledge of Allegiance into its proper perspective because I believe it may be the elixir that will save our country, which in turn may be the last bastion of liberty in the world. I don't recommend we indoctrinate our kids, but I do support immersing them in a sense of "pride of ownership." To recapture the naked patriotism that some misguided educators have purposely stripped from their souls.

As a little guy, I stood every morning with my hand over my heart to recite the Pledge of Allegiance. It made me proud I was lucky to be born American. As I grew, I wondered if children in other countries practiced similar rituals every day? I knew one thing for sure, their country didn't provide liberty and justice for all.

None of it really meant much to me until I joined a little league team and before every game, we sang the National Anthem and recited The Pledge Allegiance. When we took the field, I felt a sense of pride and was inspired to play hard to try to win every game. Not to beat my opponent, but to reaffirm my dedication and brotherhood with my teammates. They were my second family.

Our family has always been extremely close. I knew if it ever became necessary, I would lay down my life to protect my mom and dad or my brother. No questions asked, right or wrong, I needed to be there for them just as they had always been there for me.

During the Vietnam conflict I was of draft age and I wrestled with the moral dilemma of sending young men to battle indigenous villagers in the jungles of their backyard. But one thing kept coming back to me: I respected those who chose to go. They were my brothers and, right or wrong, I needed to be there for them, as I am sure they felt, they were there for me.

Subsequent life changing events, marriage and children, my mom and my best friend both succumbing to cancer in midlife, brought my worldview into focus. My immediate family, my teammates, my American citizenship, they were in effect, all the same thing. It was just a matter of scale. My allegiance, and my sense of responsibility, were inter-wound around my need to belong.

To the best of my knowledge, a sense of belonging is as basic a human need as sex. It is a fundamental drive that functions as a survival mechanism, promoting things like self-sacrifice which ultimately supports the greater need. It is what separates civilized societies from barbarian tribes.

Patriotism could just as well be called "Family-ism", because that is what it means to me.

As kids, we were raised to believe we lived in the greatest country on earth. We still celebrate our freedom on the 4th of July by watching fireworks. That is something every kid on the planet remembers every year! Watching bombs burst in mid-air leaves a powerful psychological impression. It instills a sense of pride, power and justice!

Like our own birthday, which for kids is the most personal celebration of life, the 4th of July is America's Birthday. It is the symbol of what makes America great, that it is the father figure, the provider and protector of our freedom. And the beacon of liberty for everyone on the planet.

As a kid, the word freedom didn't really have much impact unless you don't live in America. Freedom is meaningless if you have never lived in its absence. But for most of us, as we grew older, the truth about, and the impact of freedom slowly came into focus.

The day I got my driver's license is one of those freedom defining moments, at least for me. It was the day I became an adult as far as I was concerned, because it allowed me to be mobile, to set my own agenda, to show my ability to manage my time, and to be responsible for my own actions.

For each of us, those landmarks, those special occasions that marked accomplishments, like bar mitzvahs, graduations, Christmas gatherings of the extended family, those moments in time that put a lifetime into perspective, are what makes our lives rich and textured.

Standing in line at the Department of Motor Vehicles to get your license is one of those transformative moments.

Now we live in a world of incredible intensity: everything seems to be happening at a breakneck speed. With modern day technology, television, the internet, and the increased ease of travel, we are experiencing those landmarks at a dizzying rate. Since the whole world is only a click away, there are literally dozens of landmark occasions daily. Through Facebook, we can share five birthdays today!
Do you get where I am going with this? What is so special about anything anymore? Been there, done that.

Today, we are faced with unconventional wars. We are confronting everything from radical Islamic fundamentalism to the war on drugs. We fight wars on gangs, alcoholism, sexism, racial discrimination, and poverty. It seems Americans are in a perpetual state of warfare.

Our attentions are divided amongst an endless number of media choices. There is no one media channel to disseminate a compelling message of unity.

Keeping our citizens motivated to fight anything tangible is getting harder and harder, especially in the past decade of economic stagnation. It is no wonder most people are cynical of another plea to sacrifice self-interests to fight, to defend, what we all take for granted.

Like Roosevelt, our leaders have an uphill battle. Exactly where should we put our resources to work first? How should we prioritize our efforts? How much can we ask of our citizens? And most importantly, what happens if our citizens decide they won't contribute anymore? They figure they are paying enormous amounts of tax, that it is somebody else's job to do.

Oh, and by the way, there are significant numbers of Americans who have grown to *hate* our country. They live here, benefit from all of our wealth and freedom, but still hold America responsible for most of the misery in the world. And, they feel obligated to do something about their grievances, so they are actively working to undermine our constitutional conventions as we speak.

When you combine the forces of international conflict with the internal movement to dismantle the existing infrastructure of American government institutions, you have a severe case of cancer growing throughout our culture.

This disease has been present since the end of the Cold War, but it has shown only benign symptoms, that have gone mostly under the radar as we have been living the good life and not really paying much attention.

It has been subtle, but the effort to destroy patriotism has been going on for decades.

I remember a seminal moment in my senior year at Cal State University at Long Beach: I was selected to participate in an intercampus social studies exchange. I was sent to University of Southern California campus in Los Angeles, to spend a day attending a series of lectures and interactive workshops about the counterculture.

It turned out to be a kidnapping.

I was held hostage to a group of very hostile Black Panther-types who subjected me and my all-white classmates to a classic Communist re-education indoctrination campaign. I was chastised for being a "privileged middle-class white male sexist pig" who needed to recognize how my heritage had infected the world with genocide and xenophobia. That the American male was targeted for extinction and the only way to save the world was to join the underground movement to dismantle Imperialist America.

I felt lucky to get out of there alive. The experience was a turning point in my life because it forced me to look closer at what my assumptions were based on. I started to listen closer to the leftist dogma of the anti-war crowd. I didn't like what I was hearing.

Later that year I got into a heated argument with my biology teacher when she claimed human beings were scientifically no different than any other animal species. That by giving human life more value than other creatures we were violating the natural order and wreaking havoc on the environment. This was, though I didn't know it at the time, the precursor to the climate change, radical environmentalist, animal-rights movement. I was beginning to see the trend of a humanist, anti-Christian, anti-capitalist, Marxist ideological element present in every aspect of the generic anti-war movement. My eyes were opening, and my mind was reeling. I started to become disillusioned with all of the "love generation" thing.

So this stuff has been gestating for decades. Our schools, especially our colleges, have been overrun by, and are operating as, the central command posts for the radical left. They are actively working to indoctrinate and motivate the younger generations to hate America and the values we stand for.

As young people, we start out promising to protect and to serve our precious home, the good old US of A. As we mature, we naturally start to question authority and therefore some of the assumptions our promises are based upon.

In America, most of us strive to attend college. It is at that point, for many Americans, our confidence, our patriotism, and our commitments are seriously challenged.

In today's world, it is easy to become disenfranchised and disenchanted. Estranged from our community, the result is divisiveness and a loss of esprit de corps. College age youth are particularly vulnerable. They are mostly poor, have no roots or serious allegiances, and are still trying to find their way in the world.

The worldwide Communist movement figured that out right after they lost the Cold War. If their movement was to survive, they had to settle into a place that was safe from scrutiny, a place that had a sense of sanctity and authority. What better place than right in the heart of America, the college campus. Plus, the idea that colleges are sacrosanct, free from influence, and places of inquiry, study and exploration of alternative ideas fit the template of the left perfectly. Since they couldn't win the war of influence by building walls, maybe they could win the war of ideas by brainwashing young, impressionable minds.

For the past five decades, our institutes of higher learning have been thoroughly transformed into institutions of advanced Marxist-Leninist indoctrination. The evidence is clear; look at the divide in political trends. The older the citizen, the more likely they are to vote Republican, or at least to be more conservative. The younger the voter, the more likely they are to associate with the Democrats or at least to be more liberal or progressive.

Hence, we have a serious division of tribal identities. This is exactly what our schools are teaching: cling to your cultural differences, do not allow them to be absorbed by the dominant white male Judeo-Christian culture. If you do, you will be enslaved and exploited, just as the Native Americans were. By appealing to a youthful sense of justice, by emphasizing the negatives of our history, by exploiting the differences between cultures, the sexes, the races and other social constructs, ultra-leftist professors have successfully grown multiple generations of American misfits. And as they become social and business leaders, they have expanded their influence to divide our society into conflicting tribes of unpatriotic zombies.

As our local communities suffer, so does the larger national identity. America is slowly succumbing to the quagmire of tribal disunity so pervasive in the worst and most dysfunctional states of the world.

As we culturally divide uncontrollably, like cancer cells, our ability to maintain liberty quickly fades into a memory of better days past.

So, if this is the state of affairs in America, why would I say that the Pledge of Allegiance might be the elixir we need to stop the anti-American sentiment from metastasizing?

I say this because our efforts need to start at the bottom. We need to rescue the next generation. We may have problems recovering the people who we have already lost, but we still have the opportunity to salvage our children. But we have to act quickly and decisively. We have to go into our schools and reestablish the idea of patriotism. Wipe out the political correctness that will inevitably stand in our way.

Like a modern day GPS system, we need to give children directions they can follow. Being a patriot is no different than being a good parent! You nurture and protect your country because if you don't, you leave it the wolves!

Reestablishing Authority

The heart wrenching school-shooting mass murder in Newtown, Connecticut produced a nationwide soul-search for reasons and solutions. The ever increasing numbers of similar incidents demand action. The only question is what can we do to prevent or at least, discourage sick people from picking up guns and acting like a malevolent God with other people's lives?

We have all listened to the Politicians claim that more anti-gun legislation will save lives. Psychologists argue that childhood abuse, or a lack of proper bonding and love, could contribute to the root cause. Evangelists point to a decline in morals and civility. Educators complain of parental disengagement and denial. It's the economy, too many taxes, the absence of fathers, the influence of the media, disparity in wealth, and on and on and on.

The fact is, it's all about the recognition of authority, and I don't mean the police.

I am referring to a spiritual authority, a judgmental God, who though forgiving, is not an enabler. When a person either refuses to accept as fact that there is an immutable authority, or simply defies it, they are assuming the power of that authority for themselves. They suffer from a clinical condition, a mental illness called extreme narcissism.

First, let's define authority, and the role it plays in the development of the human mind. It is the human mind after all that mystifies us when an otherwise normal young man decides to brutally and violently register his disaffection with society at large, and his friends and neighbors specifically, by murdering them mercilessly with high powered weapons of death.

What kind of animal points a gun at another person's head, pulls the trigger, and then laughs saying, "Check out the brains!" as happened at the Columbine massacre?

Massacres are an act of power, much like the rape of a woman. It is the violent and brutal usurpation of power and the imposition of superiority over the victim. Murder is the ultimate rejection of authority because it represents the penultimate crime, the termination of another human being's life. The killer usurps the highest power, an act of God. From the view of the psychopathic perpetrator, the act is a way of adjusting the balance of power. That person is putting themselves into a bubble that is separate, and above, the ordinary, and they are claiming the power to determine life and death.

Authority is the ultimate power to which an individual must answer. In order to truly be authority, it's power must be immutable. However, without the power of enforcement, it is helpless to govern. In other words, in a free society such as ours, the people of the state must recognize authority voluntarily. Anything less is anarchy.

Politically, or socially, we elect our representatives, and then empower them to make laws by which we all live. Those who challenge authority, in our country, face the rule of law, where a document like the Constitution of the United States is invested with the power of authority, and enforced by mortal human beings in the justice system, to act as the standard by which society rules itself. The court system, along with an intricate network of support systems such as law enforcement, schools, church and civil organizations and associations, taxation and regulations, all act to manage our social actions.

But individually, recognizing authority is a different dynamic.

The fact is that no single social authority figure or organization can do that job alone. In fact, the old proverb applies, that absolute power corrupts absolutely. If left solely in the hands of mortals, total power will inevitably end in corruption. Outside of the social and political spectrum, life is ordered by some sense of perspective, by a personal moral code, or what is commonly described as a belief system.

That is why a higher authority is required and it must gain its power from a voluntary public. It is the very nature of the tenuous balance between all of the aforementioned elements that contribute to the success of modern society; a place where citizens can have enough freedom to feel connected to, and responsible for, the well-being of the community.

It's what is commonly called the democratic system of justice. It is not perfect; in fact, we all know how imperfect it can be. At some time in our lives, we all rail against the system.

What happens when the balance of authority is disrupted and the system breaks down? In extreme cases of a state or nation, or society, the result is usually a revolution; a violent reorganization of power. In the case of an individual, or of a small group of like-minded individuals, the result can be anything from passive resistance and civil disobedience to violence. This can range from simple civil disobedience to a revolutionary insurgency to civil war.

It could take the shape of Jihad. Terrorist organizations can cite you chapter and verse of their convoluted and passionate rationale for their bloody assaults. Many times, the perpetrators are so dispirited, conflicted or convoluted, that the outcome of their protests is suicide.

With no exceptions, terrorist actions never get the desired results. Terrorism, in and of itself, is not a political force for change. It is an act of disobedience, or defiance of authority. It is the ultimate self-indulgence. It creates fear, anger, disruption, news headlines, and any number of reactions, but other than an exchange of hostages or some promise of action, nothing concrete ever changes!

There are no wonders of the world erected by terrorists!

As for the individual, what happens when authority is disaffected or abandoned? History tells us that human beings succeed when they answer to, and live under a higher authority. In fact, the founders of our nation recognized that without some sort of support from, and a general belief in, a superior authority, their dreams of a self-regulated and free society would never be realized. Regardless of which religion you look at, all of them stress the need to believe in a higher, benevolent authority. Why? Because we also know from history, that human beings, when allowed to operate with no authority, like an astronaut without a tether, will drift recklessly, and usually, if not always, turn destructively narcissistic.

This is one of those "truths" civilized nations learned over millenniums.

In terms of our collective soul, what can society do to maintain the tenuous balance of power that keeps its citizens empowered to cooperate and contribute to an environment of peace and community? The answer is to encourage and support the recognition of an even higher authority. Yes, the recognition and support of citizen's participation in some form of subjugation, or, if you will, religion. Or, if that is too onerous for you, at least a well-defined "belief system", that recognizes and enforces some tenets of self-control determined by an authority figure.

But that "religion" must be able to function outside of government, in a vacuum of influence from any political, financial or otherwise self-interested force or forces. Whatever force it represents must trust the individuals to be able and willing to freely subjugate themselves. Some religions do not work well in a free environment. Islam, for example, requires a theocracy, a top down structure combining the theories of the religion with the enforcement abilities of the government.

The fact is, that no civilization has ever been more successful than the current Western Civilization founded on Judeo-Christian principles, which is solely responsible for our constitutional form of government where the rights and freedoms of the individual are respected and placed above that of the State, but not above everything. In fact, it even says so in the Pledge of Allegiance, "One Nation, under God..."

How does this all relate to the epidemic of youthful violence in and towards our schools, and in our inner cities? Take a serious look at the common denominator in the personality profiles of every sadistic killer; they are all incredibly narcissistic. They believe that everyone is against them, that they don't get enough respect, that hope for their future is gone, and they show no remorse, should they fail to commit suicide during their act of terrorism.

Their world is dark and inward looking. They wallow in self-pity, anger and resentment. And as a result, they elevate themselves to a position of total independence. Freedom from all civil controls and expectations, free from all judgmentalism or accountability. They end up in an empty space not even their self-involvement can adequately fill. To a world that revolves around them, and them only.

Most do commit suicide, because that is the ultimate act of self-idolatry and rejection of the authority of society.

Those who survive, when interviewed, focus all of the attention on themselves, their feelings of mistreatment and disillusionment, as though they were the victims of some tragedy. The culture of "victimology" permeates not only the psychology of the perpetrators, but is often pandered to by the morally confused educational establishment and their well-trained media.

The result of which is a self-perpetuating dynamic of high media visibility which attracts the attention of other similarly affected lost souls, who then use the "celebrity" to feed their insatiable need for exacting pain and suffering on the world they cannot otherwise control.

The turning point in the victim's' misdirected lives comes when their anger and resentment of "unrecognized" authority reaches a point of separation from reality. This is the very definition of narcissism, when the line between self-loathing and self-idolatry cross. Narcissism is essentially a psychological defense system gone mad. The individual begins to reign over all aspects of authority outside of themselves, allowing them to set new standards or to eliminate old values, such as the value of human life. Having never established respect for, or having abandoned a belief in, a higher authority, the narcissist appoints himself God.

Running Stop Signs

In terms of our nation, or the state, the insidious decay of respect for authority can be as innocuous as ignoring the speed limit of 55 mph, or just running a stop sign because you can. My mother used to call it "Little White Lies." Her theory was that the more often you lie, deceive or fudge the rules, the easier it gets and the more likely your behavior will escalate. For most healthy adults, this kind of behavior may remain benign. But when incorporated in the formative stages of childhood as a strategy to avoid authority, it becomes insidious, and very dangerous.

Kids are taught from the earliest grades to respect every rule, no matter how inconsequential it may seem. Then, as they grow older, their parents, or their surrogates, begin to set bad examples; I run a yellow light when I should've slowed, my kids notice. I make derogatory or sexist jokes, my kids notice. The President tells lies of convenience, the whole nation notices.

The hypocrisy we display towards our children is institutionalized in our schools; Isn't it revealing, that under current school rules, kids can wear virtually anything to school, T-shirts displaying foul language or X-rated graphics or present a classroom video project depicting the ritualistic murder of students and teachers, but if a kid walks onto the campus carrying a Bible, they can be suspended?

Our kids notice these enormous discrepancies and wonder just what is going on. In their insular world, there is no "authority" except maybe the authority of political correctness.

Certainly, nurturing a culture of respect for religious people isn't going to solve everything to do with violence. There is a certain amount of culpability to all of the various social and economic forces: The media hypes violence and intrigue way too much. Much of today's advertising glorifies rejection of authority. Punk rock, rap and urban music all feed on the disillusionment from, and growing disrespect for, authority. The news media puts bad news at the top of the headlines, because they want to draw a crowd. And because we live in such good times, entertainment has to outdo itself to stay ahead of the ever increasing amount of leisure time we all have, so it pushes the envelope, exploiting all the gruesome and unexplored cavities of our minds...the kids notice these things, and, unfortunately, all too often, the detrimental effects it has on their attitudes about life, are dismissed as "growing pains" or unfair over-reactions to "today's youth culture".

Have you noticed the preponderance of post-apocalyptic, dystopian movies recently? Audiences seem to be mesmerized by watching dramas about what life will be like just before and immediately after their death and the destruction of life as we know it.

What we saw happen in Newtown is a symptom of the moral vacuum that has insidiously infected our modern western civilization. We have become drunk on our own freedom, and lost sight of the responsibilities we have to something bigger than ourselves and our state. And those young men who are operating in the outer limits of tortured self-hatred succumb to the temptation to act on their own, not-so-benevolent God.

Our baby-boomer generation, in an understandable, but perhaps misguided attempt to protect citizens from religious indoctrination, has allowed the social and legislative pendulum to swing too far toward the total elimination of religious influence altogether. We have cultivated an anti-authority environment that is now producing some hideous emotionally bankrupt monsters.

Young people are particularly susceptible to the feelings of emptiness and abandonment that stems from the moral vacuum. They are looking to find their identity in their formative years, to establish a persona to wrap themselves in, as a shield from the harsh realities of the outside world. Even the most balanced, morally anchored teenagers struggle with emotional challenges and growing pains.

However, a child with no moral foundations, who has learned their standards from parents who determine their morals based on their convenience of the moment, has no chance of escaping the alluring cesspool of self-destruction. So they gravitate towards others like themselves who can give them a sense of belonging. As a direct response to their perceived rejection by society as a whole, they typically adopt anti-social images, practices and group associations (the Oakland Raiders, the Hell's Angels, etc.).

Within the middle-class, the utter contempt for authority of "White Power" Skinheads, the Wall Street Occupiers, the Black Lives Matter and Black Panthers, ISIS and Boko Haram are no different than the attraction of inner city (and more recently middle-class) kids to gangster rap, death metal bands, gang clothing, and extreme entertainment like violent pornography, freestyle kick fighting and zombie mayhem. Some of our children are drifting into the moral vacuum because they can find no reason to respect religion or authority.

In their mind, the authority society tries to impose is corrupt. The authority their parents try to impose is hypocritical, and they haven't established a relationship with any higher authority, so they turn to themselves and their like-minded brethren, for guidance.

This vacuous personality profile fits most mass murders and terrorists too.

It doesn't take a rocket scientist to note the obvious; none of the shooters in the rash of school or theatre massacres had a strong relationship with God. Terrorist organizations, though some represent hybrid, distorted religious groups, are not part of the everyday community attending church and holding Bible study classes. Narcoterrorists pray to the lord of the smugglers, the keeper of the money-chest. Western culture terrorists, gangsters and violent civil protesters are drawn to the extreme violence as a way to bond with those with similar anxieties.

Note that these gangs, cults and cliques are all as exclusionary as the groups in the greater society that they portend to hate; if you don't think, dress and act like them, you can't join up. They become what they hate, hierarchies. That should give us a clue.

In fact, if you look carefully, and listen to what they say, terrorist groups and gangs represent the new authority to their members; supplanting the missing leadership of fathers, parents, loved ones, and, yes, intangible authority, like God, in their lives.

I am not a deeply religious person myself, but what I did learn from my Sunday school years was that the Bible cautioned us not to pray to another God; that self-idolatry was a sin. Over the years I have wondered what many of the principles of any religion were based on. I think now it is pretty obvious that it is experience, thousands of years of it. Those who ignore history, and unfortunately, that is a significant number of us baby boomers and millennials, are doomed to repeat it.

If we look at some of the most persistent and troubling problems of our times, the news stories that dominate the headlines come directly from the abandonment of the Ten Commandments:

- Do not worship other Gods (celebrity worship and materialism)
- Do not create or serve idolatry (Ben Laden, Jim Jones, Scientology, Big Government)
- Do not use the Lord's name in vain (vulgarity in lyric, movies, humor)
- Keep Sunday holy (NFL/ Sports, shopping, decline in church attendance)
- Honor both parents (mutated family structures, single parenting, ageism)
- Do not murder (value human life, in the womb or the inner city)
- Do not commit adultery (marriage is impugned, sex is treated as a recreational activity)
- Do not steal (excludes governments, disadvantaged, financial scandals)
- Do not bear false witness (Facebook, Twitter, reality TV)
- Do not covet (the politics of envy, victims)

A recent court ruling required a high school to pull down a canvas sign that said, "God Bless America!"

It is shocking that we cannot hang the Ten Commandments on the walls of our schools because of the supposed conflict with the separation of church and state doctrines. Why does our generation refuse to accept wisdom from our forefathers?

Signal Lost

Why is it so hard for people to see the elephant in the room?

As a culture we doggedly focus on the wrong symptoms. No wonder why we misdiagnose all of our cultural illnesses. If you have a headache, rubbing an analgesic on your feet isn't going to reduce your pain.

In trying to understand the recent spate of mass murders, we are looking in all the wrong places.

The issue of mass murders committed by young, disenchanted men, using high power firearms is the subject of much speculation: What causes these people to take such inhumane actions to gain notoriety to cover their anger and pain for being different? Is it poverty and class envy?

Is it the effects of bullying or sexual identity conflict? Is it despair over the loss of control or social dominance? Is it the easy accessibility of cheap handguns, the nefarious influence of the NRA, or just the right wing emphasis on ignoring the plight of the underclass?

The problem with that reasoning is that all of these conditions exist for millions and millions of people who never commit heinous human executions.

So the answer is none of the above.

The elephant in the room is the "killer" profile, which on the surface, appears to be uniquely normal young men. They have friends, they attend school or at least have recently been involved in regular public activities. Yes, they are often loners, but they seldom have a history of arrests or violence. They are typically products of broken homes, with a history of bizarre and self-centered abusive behavior, and who are almost always spoiled/abused by single or separated parents who have no idea of how to temper selfish actions that show no concern for others, for norms or authority, and who substitute their friendship and coddling, or conversely their anger and psychological abuse, for parental nurturing and discipline.

Add into that petri dish our cultural devaluation of marriage and the formation of the nuclear family as an iconic and imperative tradition of child-rearing. Throw in socially accepted disrespect for unborn children, the institutionalization of abortion and the "new normal" acceptance of child abandonment by career seeking mothers and overtly ambitious father's. Then toss in widespread abuse of drugs and alcohol and the substitution of human care by television, nannies, and digital diversions, and you get self-involved, petulant and overly sensitive young men who have a chip on their shoulder and a need for acting out in extremely violent ways to attract attention.

The message these admittedly ill young men get is, "Who cares about you and your problems? You are just an obstacle to our pleasure! We gave birth to you, what else do you want from us"?

Stitch this all together, and you get a Young Franken-killer!

The new normal pattern of early abandonment by career ambitious parents, further eroded by angry, disparaging left-wing academia, has insidiously pulled the floor out from under many mentally discouraged and/or impaired boys who are going through the evolution from adolescence to manhood, historically a challenging and unpredictable life changing period. In our youth oriented culture, manhood is elusive and ill defined, and then popularly trashed as a convention of male misogyny. Unstable boys are left to navigate a dark and threatening landscape of unknown performance expectations, loneliness and disillusionment. In some cases, they are given psychoactive mood altering drugs that can have devastating side effects including hallucinations and suicidal tendencies.

No wonder these confused boy-killers are irrational!

Mass murder by young men is only one of many subjects our media completely misrepresent. Either through ignorance, apathy, or in most cases due to a cultural practice of historical miseducation and purposeful twisting of the facts to push a social agenda, and to deflect blame. These journalists come from the same generation of leaders in "modern child development" and educational egalitarianism. Today's so-called "enlightened" educators and writers taught in the halls of our hijacked advanced educational system, have been convinced they are destined to reinvent and culturally advance a generation that has been moribund by their outdated conservatism and Judeo-Christian hegemony. It is in their purview to promote and justify asymmetrical lifestyles, single and helicopter parenting, recreational drug use, sexual multiplicity, humanism, and all kinds of self-centered activities that have historically been viewed as irresponsible, and, well, ungodly.

Parents rationalize that we gave them everything, that we loved them unconditionally, and that we are proud of their achievements! Just look at all the awards posted on their Facebook pages! Sorry if we have little time to play, but we have to make a living!

Everything would be OK, we think, if we had more gun control, free access to drugs, healthcare, food, housing, education, computers and cellphones, and less prehistoric judgmentalism of modern concepts of gender, family and religion. If our capitalist society was more tolerant, generous and less focused on materialism, maybe these loner-killers could fit in better...

I read a story recently about how ageism persists in the workplace. It claimed that the U.S. Equal Employment Opportunities Commission received a little over twenty thousand charges of age discrimination in 2014, which, according to the report, means millennials are eager to enter the workforce while baby boomers are also eager to not leave the workforce.

Boomers should be going quietly into retirement, but no, the stubborn bastards are trying to hang on! How selfish! This attitude accurately reflects the dominance of the youth culture, the arrogance that "We know best because we are the best educated generation ever!" Millennials meantime, having graduated with the equivalent of a high school level education from the local college, can't seem to qualify for the job those boomers should be vacating. They face unreasonable judgmentalism from corporate America, and lifestyle limits they are simply not willing to give up for self-sufficiency (like tattoos on their face).

Why are we unwilling to admit our child rearing inventions have backfired? The now well established curriculum of pushing high self-esteem, noncompetitive collaboration and non judgmentalism has produced a generation of narcissistic kids who can't deal with adversity or workplace competition, or accept authority. They are insecure about their sexuality, their reason for being and their ability to relate to human love. They act as though they are at the end of their tether. That they have lost their psychological GPS signal.

Extreme narcissists committing mass murder is the "canary in the coal mine" of our Western Civilization. It is a series of symptoms of what the loss of respect for real authority is going to cost us in the long run. Like the decline of the Roman Empire, our kids are bearing witness to the slow decay and ultimate destruction of western civilization from within. Mass murder is the dead canary, a symbol of the lack of oxygen left in our faith-based human experiment called America.

Every time we witness another school-place massacre, we bump into that elephant again.

Backseat Driver

Remember the classic *Everyone Loves Raymond* series episode where Robert complains (and exposes the ongoing storyline) that when the family went on a road trip, they thought so little of Robert that after driving off and leaving him at a gas station rest stop, it took them hours to notice he wasn't in the car?

Robert represents the universal second child in most families who grows up feeling discounted, neglected, overlooked and in some ways abused. In many families the first born tends to be an overachiever, and as in my family, the second born, an under achiever. No matter how much I achieved, it was always in second place to my brother, just as Robert was to Raymond.

It may hold true for others in the family line, I don't know because my brother and I were the only two children. But one thing about our family, that I always cherished, was the respect both of us had for the authority and leadership of our parents. I now know that my older brother felt slighted as a young man. Even though he excelled in everything he tried, scholastically, in organized sports, and later in business, he secretly felt that mom loved me more. He revealed this painful truth to me after both of our parents were gone and in a moment of nostalgia fueled by a half dozen beers.

I would've bet she felt the opposite, but overall we both knew how dear we were to both of our folks and that they would never fail to be there for us in a time of need. They had always attended every milestone event, most if not all sports events, graduations, awards ceremonies, you name it, if it had to do with my brother or me, they were there. Both of them.

Up until their last day on earth, I would never hesitate to get their point of view, their recommendations, to tap into their vast wealth of knowledge and experience before I made any major decisions in my life. I may not always agree with them, but I also knew they had developed their perspectives with many more years of experience, and I would be a fool to discount that.

But more universally, Robert's perceived disrespect by his family represents the sense of loss felt by many of us boomer generation parents. Our children, it seems, don't need us anymore. We get a sinking feeling that young people don't place much value on our experience or, for that matter, the generations of human existence that preceded them? Do they really think that their college experience makes them the smartest person in the room?

If you have ever watched Stephen Colbert or Bill Maher, you can't help but get that message! It is easy to suggest that those that cling to traditions are just plain ignorant.

I ask because it seems the news is filled with startling social changes that fly in the face of history. I feel like our children are leaving their parents behind at the rest stop. And it isn't clear as to whether they will ever discover that we are not in the car with them.

We are all passengers on the planet earth as it travels through time and space, but those who are now holding the steering wheel seem to be driving us all over a cliff! I hate acting like a backseat driver, but when you are sitting in the back and the driver is not looking ahead, it is dark and he has no headlights on, and we are barreling down the road at 100 miles an hour, on a road I know ends at a cliff, what am I supposed to do?

Let's take the institution of marriage for example. One of the oldest institutions known to humankind. The social tool used to bind males and females together to stabilize the incredibly important and complicated function of procreation. Is there another institution on Earth that is so commonly derided on TV as marriage and the nuclear family? The declining numbers of committed male-female marriages are startling. If you listen to academia, to pop cultural discussions, if you look at home buying trends, at mortgage applications, you can't help but be alarmed at the declining numbers of the institution as we have known it.

The birth rate, around the world, is plunging. In a time when people are living longer healthier lives, women, for whatever reason, are losing their maternal instinct to get married and have children.

Arguably one of the most enduring social constructs, marriage is endemic to all civilized societies. It extends to every corner of the planet, regardless of race, creed, color or religious association. Cultures with non-traditional organizational structures, non-religious groups, and even prehistoric tribes living in complete isolation, practice marriage rituals. Literally hundreds of previous generations have exalted, venerated, even worshipped marriage.

Every scientific study ever produced about marriage shows it has mostly positive effects on the individuals involved, on the offspring, and within the community. It bridges racial and religious divides. Marriage supports the idea of community cohesion, peace and stability, and integration of people with different backgrounds and cultural variations. It helps communities, schools, churches, and social networks build identity. It supports the protection and nurturing of children.

It might just be the most important cultural institution in the history of Mankind. It is under assault by many leftwing groups.

So now, our children are convinced that it should be abandoned and a new, much different template that they have devised should replace it. I am not interested in making judgments', just in pointing out the implied disrespect and dismissal of timeless cultural institutions that we are witnessing at an alarming rate today. I would not be so concerned if we were talking about how we set up our schools, or cut our hair. But messing with something as socially endemic as marriage, pulling the rug out from under such a structurally important leg of civilization is a bit presumptuous.

Let's look at patriotism. Can I mention it, or would that be too incendiary? Am I displaying my parochialism? Is it inherently warlike to express an allegiance to my country? You would think so if you listened to college professors, or many of the leftist millennials who have been taught at the institutions of higher learning in America, and I might add, throughout the western world.

What was inculcated as a social and civic bond at the earliest stages of my life, is now characterized as a tool of white male misogyny and privilege and the exploitation of the poor to send minorities and poor boys to war over oil and white owned corporate interests. Traditional symbols of patriotism like the flag, or wearing military uniforms, or a lapel pin, are often targets of derision and shame expressed by young people who have an idealistic view that if we just gave up our borders, lowered our flags, avoided conflict, and showed less pride in our country and its dubious accomplishments, there would be less rancor and war. This ideological wistfulness is a symptom of a serious social illness that will manifest itself in the future.

Then there is the concept of American Exceptionalism: the term is deemed to be an arrogant, self-serving construct to elevate the United States to a pinnacle that is undeserved, incendiary, and condescending.

It ignores, however the obvious facts that America has been and still is the beacon of Freedom around the globe. That America has saved more people from totalitarianism than all other counties combined. That the presence of American military might has for over one hundred years secured independence and provided security from instability, violence, and genocide for most of mankind.

It ignores the obvious fact that without exception, countries that have engaged in war with us inevitably end up better off after their defeat than before. No other world power can make that claim, which in itself qualifies America for the brand of "exceptional".

Some in our culture embrace a blame-America-first-mentality because it is supported by a Marxist leaning cabal of University professors and intellectual elitists. President Obama, a Harvard graduate, spent much of his first term traveling around the world apologizing for America's mistakes in the past. He epitomizes the growing consensus that America is responsible for most of the misery in the world because we have been arrogant, selfish and insensitive to other nations and cultures. Our consumer mentality, resulting from unfettered capitalism, has "raped" the world of its resources, contaminated the environment, warmed the globe, and institutionalized racism and poverty.

The sad truth is; how can you blame our children for adapting the socially accepted party line? Since kindergarten they have had this stuff pounded into their head at all levels of their education. All they hear about is end-of-humanity calamities, most of which were engendered by their own country and by implication, their own parents. That would be you and me.

There are the institutions of higher education teaching global warming as "settled science". Our schools follow some simple curricula; the world is under threat from warming caused by people who drive too much, corporations who poison the environment and their customers, through a coalition of international drug companies and medical professionals, enslave them to overpriced and dangerously untested drugs. There are people who brutalize, enslave and eat animals, individuals who smoke, armies who kill for oil, and all of this is orchestrated by white men who make all the wrong decisions for women, and abhor homosexuals.

When your kids come home from college, they aren't the same. You're lucky if they will ever speak to you again.

Yes, I am a white male, so maybe I am a little paranoid, but if I were the head of an Asian family, I would be equally worried. Why? Because you guys pay too much attention to scholastic accomplishment. You abuse your children by demanding too much respect for your authority.

Your extremely high rate of high school and college graduation is taking advanced educational opportunities away from inner city kids who need it most. You're domineering and selfish! And so your kids are disproportionately successful.

The war on women is worrisome. Since I am married to a woman, and my daughter has recently married, I am defensive about anyone attacking women. The problem is, according to discontented leftists, I'm the one prosecuting the war on women. I am the threat to their opportunities, to their self-respect. It is all us white males who are guilty of denying women equal pay for equal work, the pride of professional career accomplishment. Us old white guys are wrecking the lives of those that we promised to cherish and protect and those that we helped raise. It is men, who cannot get pregnant who want to manage how women should deal with an unwanted pregnancy. It is men like me who make the office environment hostile to women because we say things like, "*Honey*, you did a great job on this report!"

Current presidential candidate Hillary Clinton can't make a speech without mentioning, "I am a woman!" Not sure whether that is supposed to enlighten me or threaten me.

Suggesting men started a war on women is stupid. Men have been fighting wars long enough to know you don't start a war you can't win. Not only are us guys now the minority on the planet, but we have been totally emasculated by our youth culture. Men are increasingly becoming irrelevant, and so is our counsel. When was the last time a male was promoted to chancellor at your local university? Have you seen a male doctor lately? The next time you go to court you will probably have your case decided by a female judge.

It is counterintuitive isn't it? Watching the incredible ascension of women in the workplace speaks loudly of the failure of the war on women. It has obviously been a colossal flop. Would the war on women illustrate the law of unintended consequences? As much as we thought our baby boomer generation had wrestled with racism, sexism, poverty, war, and social injustice, it looks like we have found ourselves caught in a tide pool of disintegrating values, divided and antagonistic racial tensions, and an explosion of civil unrest, wars and cultural conflicts all around the world.

All of which can be blamed on our military industrial complex. Us older folks know about the history of wars. The barbaric battles and campaigns of the Middle Ages. The brutal and stupid waste of human life during our Civil War and then again on a more massive scale in World War I. The sickening and more modern worldwide destruction of human inventory of World War II. We learned about this in school, and through the media, movies and later TV. We listened to the stories of our forefathers and read their letters sent home, their snapshots and their news clippings. We cried when our contemporaries were killed and maimed in Korea and Vietnam. We cried when they died because we knew they gave so much and we lost so many.

And then there is Post Traumatic Stress Disorder. When we were called to serve in Vietnam, many said no--those who didn't say no were damaged for life by the experience and then they were spat upon when they came home. Instead of venerating the young men and women who gave their freedom to protect ours, many of those "Blame-America-First" anti-war activists were persuaded to paint them as animals, sent to destroy and terrorize innocent people of color. Our freedom defenders returned to a nation at war with itself, and they were made out to be symbolic of everything that was wrong with America.

Now along comes a generation who has no real-time experience with war. What they have been told in school is hindsight that is filtered through political lenses often hostile to America. The closest connection they have to real battle is the Gulf War and Vietnam, meaning it was you and me that give them their perspective. For many of us it was so unpleasant we either refuse to talk about it or we talk trash about it. In the high visibility TV enhanced worst possible scenario, someone goes berserk with an AK47 in a bell tower, and all our war veterans are painted as potential psychotic killers.

This current generation of thirty and forty somethings, and to an even greater degree those in their twenties, really believe war is preventable and that the only reason it occurs is because rich people get richer from it. That is what they have learned from college, from angry and disillusioned minority groups, and left-leaning media outlets like *KPBS*, and that narrative is reinforced every day by mainstream Hollywood. That is their answer to just about everything. If rich people didn't get richer from war, poverty, racism, disease, suppression of women, and hatred of homosexuals, then the world would be one big "Sesame Street Romper Room".

My concern is simple: how do we reverse this insidious tendency to dismiss all of the lessons of history that our youth culture ignores? How do we convince them that preserving, and respecting the cultural institutions that have proven to be valuable and important is just as important as taking credit for inventing the newest, but unproven, template for sustaining the human race?

Where did we go wrong? How did we manage to destroy our own credibility in just one or two generations? Of course we made some of the same mistakes of our parents, that goes hand in hand with the evolution of the species. All generations have to make many of the same mistakes the previous generation had to make to learn. But why try to reinvent the wheel? Not just come up with a better wheel, but toss the old one under the bus before you have any significant real world experience with the new one?

So as I sit in the backseat of my offspring's beautiful, hi-tech, hi-mileage hybrid automobile, I note that the young driver is not watching the car in front of him. That he is busy using his smartphone to text inconsequential messages to his similarly bored and disengaged friends, and as I note the road signage indicates we are rapidly approaching a dead end, in the dark, and since we are barreling along at near 100 miles per hour, you will excuse me if I make a few rather insensitive and loud noises.

Ultimately, I wish that I had been inadvertently left behind at the last gas station.

Hollywood On Your Left

Aaron Sorkin is celebrated as one of Hollywood's most prolific and talented scriptwriters. He shot to prominence as the lead writer for the Bill Clinton era hit TV show *The West Wing*. In a highly viewed YouTube scene from the movie *The Newsroom*, scripted by Sorkin, actor Jeff Daniels goes into a rant about the use of the term "American Exceptionalism".

It went viral.

In the scene, the famous newsman is lecturing a classroom full of young college students. In our college system, notable "experts" are often given the opportunity to share their experience and wisdom with students. In this scene, the national TV news anchor, portrayed by actor Jeff Daniels, is imparting his knowledge of world affairs, presumably learned from reading news scripts for many years. "There is absolutely no evidence to support the statement that America is the greatest country in the world."

After seeing this scene on YouTube, my son recommended I view it too. He said it was thought provoking. In his mind, it made sense and was shocking, because, as it was designed to do by Sorkin, it shook his patriotic foundations. I tried to explain to him that just because an actor acts well informed doesn't mean he is well informed. In the case of Jeff Daniels, I reminded my son that he was also the star of one of the most innocuous and stupid movies ever made, *Dumb and Dumber*.

In the scene from *The Newsroom*, after spouting a series of statistics about America's mediocre ranking in subjects that Liberals consider the most important social categories, such as literacy, civil rights, science, social justice, life expectancy, household income, and the all-important one, the number of incarcerated citizens per capita, Daniels concludes, "Now none of this is the fault of a twenty-year-old college student, but you are, none the less, a member of the worst generation ever. So when you ask what makes us the greatest country in the world, I don't know what the f**k you are talking about!"

Daniels definitely got the arrogance and condescension part of the news anchor's character right!

Then, Daniels, speaking directly to the students, goes on to note how he appreciates great script writing, and as an actor, how the character's monologue resonated with him.

"I remember reading it, 'you may not like it, you may not agree with it, you know--for those who are patriotic and wave the flag and don't want to hear it, but there's nothing in it that's not true--it's all true, sorry to tell you, it's all true.' So that's what resonated with me."

I guess that means he is not a patriot or a flag waver. He definitely is pissed off at his own country. And he obviously relishes the opportunity to use Sorkin's gift for dialogue to sound out his own anger.

Then he revealed his acting motivations; "To be able to say that (in a major movie), to be able to take words like the way this guy (Sorkin) can put them together and throw it at the lens, throw it at an audience, it's, for an actor, it's gold!"

Of course it is if you are a flaming, left-wing Hollyweird zealot. It is actor's gold, because it solidifies his anti-American, anti-establishment credentials in the eyes of the elite Hollywood cabal. Aaron Sorkin, as gifted as he is (and he is) has given the Hollywood left a voice. He is an articulate collaborator who is capable of verbalizing their collective anger, disillusionment and self-righteousness.

For provocateurs like Daniels, Sorkin provides the grenades to throw at the audience. It makes him feel powerful, intelligent, and places him on a pedestal for the peasants, or in this case, the students, to admire.

"Two legs bad, four legs good!" Napoleon urged the animals to rally and reject the humans, in Orwell's *Animal Farm*. The Hollywood elite pound the same message about flag wavers, patriots and conservatives, "liberals good, conservatives bad"!

So after watching the YouTube piece, I decided to offer my son another perspective. I just couldn't let the claim go unanswered. I asked my son, "What do you think about the concept of American Exceptionalism?"

He admitted it wasn't something he had given a lot of thought to. Interesting, I thought, as he was entering his fifth year of college studies, and so far, anyway, the idea had not been aired in any classroom scenario. I wasn't surprised, just concerned.

American Exceptionalism is controversial amongst academia, and in left leaning circles, because, in their mind, it promotes the myth that America leads the world in freedom and opportunity. In the minds of the blame-America-first-crowd that couldn't be further from the truth.

Is the concept of American Exceptionalism just overzealous patriotism, braggadocio, or just arrogance? Is claiming that America is the best thing to happen to the planet justified?

Absolutely.

If we look at the history of our planet, it may be hard to make that claim. History is a very long timeline. Pitting various kingdoms and empires against each other would be an exercise in futility. Each existed in different historical eras, with totally unrelated circumstances. History is a long convoluted time warp, and there is no way to compare apples with apples.

So, for the sake of this discussion, and as far as what Jeff Daniels was referring too, let us focus on the Modern Era. If the term exceptional means "unique, unusual or to stand out", then since the early part of the nineteenth century, America has been a phenomenon. In a political context, only America has established a consistent record of an advanced government organization, closely reflecting the demands, the needs and the attitudes of the electorate, all while making dramatic transitions in leadership, and social values, in a peaceful, organized manner. Only America has an environment that protects multiculturalism, pluralism, and a vast assortment of religious practices. Only in America is the term "struggle" considered safe and normal. Americans have challenged colonialism, slavery, aristocracy, social stratification. We have led the world in educating women and giving them the right to vote.

And though we are not there yet, we continue to try to achieve broad civil rights and racial equality. Something no civilized society can honestly claim to have accomplished.

Remember, when the Founding Fathers escaped religious and political persecution by the British monarchy, citizens were universally considered subjects. It was the establishment of the constitutional form of government that created "citizen voters". So when the BAF crowd suggests that other government systems offer their constituents more, they are saying what the Donkey leaders in Orwell's *Animal Farm* famously declared, "All animals are equal. But some are more equal than others."

In highly socialized countries, the kind Sorkin and Daniels idealize, the elites redistribute wealth and tell the not-so-smart guys, "you're better off now, thanks to us."

As for American imperialism and adventurism and the military industrial complex, US military intervention has, in almost every case, been a result of our moral imperative to support human rights and freedom. We may sometimes lose focus, but the motives have always been altruistic: our militias fight to keep our people and our allies from subjugation. The US hasn't annexed another country since the Mexican-American War, in 1848. Not exactly Modern Times...

Finally, I challenge anyone to show me a record of victorious benevolence like ours. In all of the wars we have fought in the Modern Era, our Civil War, WWI, WWII, the Vietnam War, the Korean War, the Gulf War, you name it, there is one undeniable truth: In victory, all of our adversaries are better off today than they were before the conflict. Japan, Germany, Italy, and Vietnam, are all thriving, and for the most part, socially and economically advanced societies. Yes, Iraq is still a mess, but that conflict was not, and is not, being fought as a war. It is only a response to civil disobedience, in collaboration with an inept and indifferent puppet government and a civil population so completely decimated that the concept Iraq as a country has all but evaporated.

President Obama has said, when asked if he believed in the concept of American Exceptionalism, "I believe in American Exceptionalism just as I suspect the Brits believe in British exceptionalism and the Greeks believe in Greek exceptionalism."

President Obama, always the egalitarian, may not fully understand the term, because by its very nature there can only be one "exceptional" anything. But he was, apparently implying the Greeks had, hundreds of years before the birth of Christ, incorporated the earliest tenets of basic human rights, and promoted individual citizen's responsibilities, in their civic organizational ideas and city states. And that the British Empire had literally ruled the world for decades.

But few historians would suggest that modern history has experienced a more widespread positive impact than the establishment of the representative republic of the United States of America. There has never been anything like it in the history of humanity. Though it is only just under three hundred years old, our unique American experiment in liberty and self-government, is and will for the foreseeable future, be the template all governments of freedom loving men and women will attempt to emulate.

If you only look at a statistical matrix of the social categories cited by Sorkin, it is hard to say America is number one in the world. But like any statistical analysis, the numbers can be misleading. For example, what other country on the planet has the cultural diversity of the US? There are no countries with remotely similar numbers, per capita, of the incredible melting pot of backgrounds, all living together in relative peace. This fact alone affects all of the other measurement data, because we are not a homogenous society. Educating hundreds of different racial and social groups is different than working with people who all speak the same language, have similar cultural values and social, religious and racial experiences. Nations like Japan, or Norway, have little or no cultural, linguistic or racial diversity.

The idea that our schools rank lower than other countries is contrary to common sense; why are our schools overflowing with foreign students? China sends literally hundreds of thousands of their leaders' children to America for advanced degrees.

Why do so many outsiders want their kids educated here? I would suggest our diversity, our populism, our support and history of "out-of-the-box" thinking, our entrepreneurial spirit. Our history of free discussion, even revolutionary attitudes, are not available anywhere else in the world. These also make the application of educational studies challenging. Parents of inquisitive youngsters from all over the world see tremendous value in exposing their kids to the American experience.

The brightest students from all over the globe are eager to attend our institutions of advanced learning. Because of our diversity, American Universities are among the highest rated in the world.

The same principles hold true with our medical services. Wealthy people travel thousands of miles to access American hospitals for advanced medical treatment unavailable in their own countries.

The all-important issue of the rate of incarceration in America, always cited by the BAF crowd, is also one of those shocking statistics that must be properly framed to make much sense. First of all, Americans are free spirits! Breaking the law is no big deal. We nurture and encourage a natural suspicion of authority from a very early age. For most people, cheating on their taxes is an acceptable practice. We have large populations who use recreational drugs with impunity. In other societies, breaking any law, as inconsequential as we may seem it to be, is considered a serious offense. At an early age, children raised in other countries learn to conform. Americans reject conformity. Americans are all children of the Wild West. And, there aren't too many countries that have a legal system based on the concept that you are innocent until proven guilty, so more people are inclined to take legal risks.

Our pop culture creates opportunities to become a criminal starting at very young ages and at some point, law enforcement has no choice but to incarcerate repeat offenders. Yes, American jails are full of prisoners, but there are very few of them who got sent there after their first offense. So, is our legal system overly punitive, or are our citizen's slow learners? I would argue our system is too eager to give second chances, which ultimately promulgates anti-authoritarian attitudes.

The whole inner city subculture of gangs and rap music, the "Gangsta" lifestyle promotes anti-authoritarianism. In these deviant antisocial circles, having served time is considered a badge of honor.

This raises the question of recidivism. In America, 7 out of 10 released from prison will be rearrested within five years. This indicates a serious problem with reintegration. For many prisoners, the reason they became criminals in the first place is they were unable to thrive within the law. They ventured into criminal enterprises and once released find they have no alternative but to go back to their previous lifestyle. This is a failure of the system to prepare these people to *Turn Right at Lost*.

But I digress...

So what definitively makes America so unique?

Many WWII vets and historians will say that without the help of America, the Allies simply could not have defeated both the Nazis and the Japanese.

Which country can be counted as the foremost enemy of Communism, the ideological enemy of democracy and pluralism? Which country has shown a consistent willingness to step in to stop Communist takeovers of small countries like Vietnam, South Korea, and Nicaragua? Which country traditionally donates more resources to mitigate world poverty, disease and natural disasters? Which country has developed, and is leading major scientific achievements in agriculture, in medicine, in communications and research?

As inflammatory and biased as Sorkin's script and Daniels rant are, they are also void of serious analysis. They are reflective of the knee jerk rhetoric of angry liberals who must suffer from a deep guilt complex, because it is otherwise impossible to reconcile their extreme wealth, business success, and ability to say whatever they want with their disillusioned rejection of their motherland.

CHAPTER FIVE

Tribal Traffic

You would never know that listening to people in the UN but Tribalism is the Father of Racism."

—Stanley Couch

Everyday People

Every election cycle, voters are once again asked to wade through and work out incredibly nuanced and complicated public policy initiatives, massive budgeting challenges, educational curricula decisions, cultural divisions, and to mitigate the latest cultural and racial outbreak.

They represent the interests of all age groups, races, religious affiliations, unions, business groups, retirees and thousands of other special interest groups. Presumably they are all concerned about and anxious to protect and nourish our great American social experiment.

I can only pray that is true...

Like the old axiom, if a story goes far enough around a table, it becomes unrecognizable by the time it returns to the starting point. The goals and aspirations of our National ambition, "One Nation, Under God, With Liberty and Justice for All" is once again, about to be tested.

We are not unlike every other nation on mother earth in one basic respect; we are a nation of tribes. Whether we have a German, Irish, British, Nigerian or Japanese ancestry, or we have been married into or been born from some hybrid racial or national marriage, we are all essentially roots of a tribe.

And, just like all other humans, Americans harbor prejudices, anger, resentments and fears about other tribes. We have, as a nation, made enormous efforts to fight racial and cultural divides, and to some degree, have had a measure of success. But the truth is, there is no escape from human nature. We are an imperfect species, so we do what we can.

The most irritating part is that for all our gallant efforts, there seems to be an intrinsic element of discontent, or perhaps, disingenuousness to the work we have put in. Somehow, some way, something always happens to sabotage even the best of intentions.

It strikes me as a self-fulfilling prophecy that racism and bigotry are permanent fixtures in the human existence, and therefore so is war. Even within a somewhat settled nation, as hard as we try to be inclusive, non-judgmental, and diverse, the existence of class and cultural unrest has never really been resolved to anyone's satisfaction.

As a young man in the sixties, I danced to *Everyday People* by Sly and the Family Stone. Never once did it occur to me that fifty years later we would still be seeing black Americans rioting in the streets of Missouri declaring, "Don't Shoot Us!", and "Black Lives Matter!"

When Marvin Gaye broke through with the mega-hit *Sexual Healing* who would have thought the divide between men and women would ever reach the proportions of anger and resentment we see today in print, TV and film, where men are consistently depicted as selfish and demented sexual predators, especially *within* marriage! Where Beyoncé would resort to donning Black Panther garb on the Super Bowl stage to pronounce her racial femininity. Where Madeleine Albright, the former Secretary of State would say, "There's a special place in hell for women who don't help each other!" implying women must vote for women or they should be considered traitors to their species.

Who would have thought? Not a young man of the enlightened sixties, that's for sure!

The anger over "Equal pay for equal work" certainly has merit, but doesn't the issue really revolve around the tribal aspect of the workplace more than the pure dominance of men over women?

How many Muslims worked at the Charlie Hebdo offices in Paris, for example?

Hierarchies develop in all kinds of cells. Within women dominated spaces, men often feel resistance to advancement. It probably isn't just, but workplaces and private groups and institutions are naturally going to revolve around founders and their selected teammates.

Birds of a feather flock together. What's wrong with that?

If you are a girl, or if you are an effeminate boy, and the Boy Scouts make you uncomfortable, don't just complain about it, start your own interest group. That is the entrepreneurial spirit of America!

It is a mountain of the highest proportions to climb, but herding Americans is like herding cats! In fact, it is more like herding cats, dogs, black widow spiders and ducks and mice. Everyone is lined up to climb aboard the ark to the future, and we are all fighting for that desirable spot at the front of the line.

There are a few hall monitors attempting to delegate some sense of order, barking out instructions, making promises, threats and offering advice, and in some cases, some solace. Though it resembles a line of impatient and sugar-charged adolescents, it is in fact our American family.

Part of our family of tribes are the Republicans. They act like dogs.

I like dogs because we have a win/win relationship. When I call my dog, she comes to me because she wants to. She needs me and I need her. We're family. Dogs want to be loved. I know a few Republican Senators who want to be loved, but they seem a little too needy. They tend to be RINOs (Republican in name only) and sometimes they are too smart for their britches.

Dogs tend to run in packs. They instinctively accept the need for order. Dogs are loyal, in the same way most Republicans are loyal to the Constitution. Like me, they are creatures of habit; when they find something works, they do it over and over, like bringing back the Frisbee. They just know you are going to throw it again!

Dogs prefer the outdoors where there is space to run, play, bark and dig. Republicans populate the wide open states like Wyoming, Utah, Arizona and Montana. Their trusty dogs help them round up cattle, ducks and geese. Republicans like to shoot guns, hunt and fish, ride horses and dig for oil.

Democrats are more like cats.

They are wild, independent and selfish. They talk about love, but are weary of it, because it means giving up some of their independence. It is the Democrats who push for gender blurring, and freedom from responsibility legislation. Legalizing marijuana, government paid abortions, and all sorts of nanny-state rules about smoking on the beach, protecting darter snails in mud puddles, are all trademarks of liberal legislatures.

Cats don't work much. Ever heard of a seeing eye cat? Cats will give up freedom for security. That's why they make great indoor pets. Give them food and comfort, a nice soft sofa to sleep on, and leave them alone, and they will be purr-fectly content.

Democrats need many group constituencies to form a coalition to win elections. Like most cats, the groups have very selfish agendas, so they wouldn't get very far if they had to win elections alone. But, like cats, Democratic constituencies are very clever; they strategically form alliances to serve their greater need, and use their group power to buy favors. Unions have learned how to herd cats; they wave dollar bills in front of them.

There are some rather telling statistics that go along with my line of thinking. A study by the American Veterinary Association found that 9 of 10 states with the highest ownership of dogs went for Romney in the 2012 election. But 4 of 5 states with the highest cat ownership went for Obama. Of course, the high density states like New York are cat states because of their urbanization.

I live in California, the state that elected Republican Governor Ronald Reagan, but that was many dog years ago. Since then the state has gone politically crazy and now we have the ultimate polecat as Governor, Jerry "Moonbeam" Brown.

In a general way, I do think the liberal analogy holds up, but where I see a significant divergence is with progressives.

I know, progressives are the new ultra-liberals. The term progressive sounds more modern, more educated, and by inference, more socially advanced. The liberal label became too pejorative, too passive, too attached to less activist leaders like Martin Luther King, JFK and Jimmy Carter.

There are still some more moderate and less obsessive mainstream Democrats, who view the world as bigger than themselves, with room for disagreement, discussion, and possibly compromise. Progressives marginalize them as relics of the past.

I believe most Democrats still view themselves as open minded, inclusive, peace-loving and engaged. Most embrace marriage, in its broadest sense. Most Democrats have Republican friends. You have seen cats and dogs that are affectionate with each other. There are many Republican/Democrat couples, Mary Matalin and James Carville for example. Their life/political strategies are diametrically opposed, but they respect each other's intellect, and give space to their differences with humility.

Where progressives differ from old school Democrats is that they aren't interested in being inclusive, tolerant or engaged. They are singular, insulated and elite. Progressives reject marriage, period.

The institution of marriage, for example, to a progressive is a prison sentence, and the job of raising children is demeaning.

Progressive writer Amy Glass thinks women are fooling themselves to think raising children is an important job or that managing a family household is anywhere near as difficult as building a professional career.

Glass stated:

> "Men don't care to "manage a household." They aren't conditioned to think stupid things like that are important...Women will be equal with men when we stop demanding that it be considered equally important to do housework and real work. They are not equal. Doing laundry will never be as important as being a doctor or an engineer or building a business."

It makes me wonder, where was her mom during Amy's formative years? Her anger and resentment and dismissive attitude toward any woman who isn't 'career' oriented gives the impression that she suffers from a sense of abandonment.

Nope, as carefree and independent as they profess to be, progressives aren't cats. Progressives are more like black widow spiders. They live in, and are perfectly happy to stay in, their homespun world. Their web of insulation allows them to ignore accountability, judgment, and standards. In fact, they associate standards with a bourgeois straight jacket, especially for women.

They may hook up with a partner for purely selfish reasons, but the relationship is doomed right from the start. At some point, the spider becomes a Black Widow, and eats her mate. It is hard to name a strongly progressive couple who have maintained a lifelong relationship.

In her piece called *Successful Women Don't Fall in Love*, Ms. Glass gleefully states:

> "I am in love with myself, in love with building my work, which will outlive me, and in love with proving people wrong, the ones who told me what I couldn't do– be happy and secure and the center of my own world."

Trees of Life

Civilization is a stand of trees all fighting for the sunlight.

To me, the recent racial violence and civil disobedience in Ferguson Missouri is just a microcosm of worldwide terrorism. If you look at the rhetoric of the Islamic terrorists, it is identical to the protestors in Ferguson, or in any other civil unrest in America or in any big city in the world.

Terrorists justify their barbarism by saying it is the only way they can be heard. They say they are disrespected and sabotaged by the infidels of the western mentality. Their peaceful religion is mischaracterized and their God is disrespected so they are forced to explode bombs in synagogues and marketplaces and kill members of their own faith, because it is all in service to a greater good. Those who don't believe as they do must be eradicated.

In Ferguson, the Black Lives Matter leaders claim that the denial of civil rights, the outright racism and murder of "innocent" young black men is indigenous to American society that is run by privileged white men who want to suppress black people and indirectly perpetuate slavery. They say those who haven't experienced slavery cannot properly understand or respect their condition.

In Afghanistan, the Taliban is fighting against the imposition of western values that threaten the order of Islamic fundamentalism and male-centric Sharia law and the complete subordination of any other religion, education, and the rights of their slaves, their women.

If we substitute the words 'peaceful religion' with the phrase 'innocent black males', you can see that the implication is the same. The core values of the 'Islamic community,' and similarly, the 'Black community' are under attack by white (Judeo-Christian) males who have all of the power and weapons at their disposal.

The Black Lives Matter movement is to the civil rights movement what the ISIS movement is to the Muslim religion. Both legitimate groups are shadowed by extremist offshoots that twist the core values of the widely respected efforts of the moderate factions. The extremists claim to be representatives of the mainstream when in fact they are perversions. And since their selfish and dark aspirations cannot win popular support, they resort to extreme strategies to destabilize their opponents. They claim that no one will listen to them if they were to work within the system.

Therefore, an asymmetric war is justified. Call it terrorism, guerrilla warfare, or civil disobedience, the results are pretty much the same: destruction of innocent people's property and lives. And those who practice it are uncivilized.

There is a lot of discussion in the media about the use of the term thug. Some say it is the new n-word. They say it implies "young black males" so therefore it is discriminatory and prejudiced to use the term when calling out the violent protesters who were trashing Baltimore.

The Mayor of Baltimore apologized because she says she spoke in generalities when she used the word to describe the people who were burning cars and breaking into stores to loot merchandise. Indeed, President Obama also called the violent people thugs, and said they are "not protesters, but agitators" who are anti-productive.

As a side note, this kind of violence occurred in Seattle a few years ago, when the violent protests were about transnational banking and the anti-Wall Street protesters were made up of all races. So the idea that Baltimore's thugs are inherently black, and therefore exempt from contempt is ludicrous.

Thugs are thugs.

I find it interesting that when the country is confronted with such ugliness, the destruction of neighborhoods, of innocent citizen's private property, and the wanton use of violence to incite more violence, many so-called social leaders divert the attention away from the criminal element and on to the use of language. It is a classic Orwellian strategy to change the subject when your position is indefensible.

It is indefensible to support anyone who commits violent crimes, for any reason! It is no different than suggesting that the Nazis had some good reasons for murdering six million people in the holocaust.

Thugs mask their antisocial behavior with complaints about disillusionment, poverty, homelessness, police brutality, abandonment and political corruption, all issues that have some element of truth and social injustice. But all subversive movements use the same moral high ground to justify their destructive reign of terror, and their demand for complete social upheaval and wealth redistribution.

I would suggest that the media is complicit in this travesty of the perversion of the language. It is exactly what George Orwell predicted, that at some point, forces of repression would co-opt the language to, in effect, rewrite the narrative to fit their template. In an effort to recruit and to create an atmosphere of anger and fear, repressive regimes, or in this case, subversive elements, need to redirect political discourse in order to frame their grievances and anger as something noble.

Our modern civilization, the tree of life, grows above ground. It flourishes in the sun and breathes the oxygen in the air. It can blossom with beauty and bring fruit to our tables. It is the essence of life and promulgation. The roots, however, grow where it is dark and they can be invasive and destructive. They tend to feed off of others and suck the vitality out of their neighbors. Some roots systems are far greater in size and reach than their above ground brothers. They survive where most other species go to die.

The world has been this way forever. We must accept there are certain realities about life that we will never change. Some people will never fit in. Some will thrive only on the misery of others and may get stronger and more extensive in their reach because there is more darkness in their world than there is light in ours.

As trees, it is our job to use the light to make more joy and to recycle the air to make more oxygen. We would be wasting our opportunity if we spend too much of our resources trying to bring the roots to the surface.

Obama Law

The events of the past couple of years regarding race in our country are very disturbing. When the presidential election results for 2008 were announced, most Americans hoped that having a black man in the White House would put aside the whole race thing so we could tackle some of the more pressing issues in the world.

Unfortunately, the exact opposite has happened.

It seems to me that my boomer generation has done more to mitigate the institutionalization of race and gender discrimination than any society or generation in the history of the planet. We increased funding for inner city schools, bused students to integrate the races, we made discrimination illegal in almost every social and business enterprise, we put quotas on graduation and scholarships, and in every possible way used media to establish a colorblind community.

We can't change human nature, so things like bigotry, ignorance and insensitivity are never going to be eliminated. But as an ideological generation, ours has worked hard to bring about racial and gender equality. Much more so than our fathers' and grandfathers' generations.

I have a very bad feeling in my stomach. I sense a creeping social trend toward a second civil war in America. It is impossible to ignore the growing chorus of unhappy, angry and hate filled people (mostly of color) who can't get passed our flawed human condition. From Missouri to South Carolina, the images are the same: some people in America hate this country and everything it stands for.

President Obama, who is himself Harvard educated, and incredibly successful, has once again articulated his outrage at "institutionalized racism" in America. He stood in front of the country and wagged his finger at us all like we were kindergarten students, and chastised us about our simplistic acceptance of views held by people like Dylan Roof, the crazy young man who slaughtered nine parishioners in South Carolina earlier this year.

Can you think of one person who has expressed camaraderie with Roof?

Ignoring all of the powerful statements of outrage across all religious and civic organizations of all races and creeds, the demonstrations of moral outrage and love and support for the victims' families, total and complete repudiation of the thoughts and actions of maniacs like Roof, our President chose to use the incident as a political stick to browbeat white Americans for what he perceives as their subliminal hatred of black people.

He didn't specifically call out white people, but who else is he referring to? He couches his comments with words like 'we' and 'us' but it is impossible to imagine he is talking to blacks. That leaves virtually everyone else! Of course he excuses blacks even though his comments were followed just a few hours later by the Ayatollah of Racists, Louis Farrakhan, who demanded his followers "bring down" the American flag because those that carry it are the same people who killed those people in that church in Charleston, and are the one's "we are fighting!"

And the African Methodist Episcopal Church audience cheered! I thought Farrakhan was a Muslim. How come he is getting cheers from a Methodist audience? More evidence that America is seriously lost...

While most media outlets mentioned his outburst and questioned his seriousness, they rather blithely accepted his bigotry as a reflection of many disenfranchised Muslims and Blacks, and went on to categorize some of the crimes Farrakhan was referring to.

It is as though the whole population has been exposed to some sort of unseen, odorless gas and is anesthetized to the degree that we are zombies. Unable to discern truth from lies, reality from fiction, honesty from deceit or love from hate. Or worse, history from construct.

The anger is growing with those of us that have been patient, tolerant, and incredibly activist. It is also simultaneously being fueled by the leader of the free world, which results in us vs. them situation where the President's supporters are dividing America into tribes, sending those who don't accept every over-the-top symbolic action to the gallows. If you aren't on board with destroying every symbol of the Confederate South, you are an apostate. Obama and his tribal supporters are acting just like the ISIS Islamist extremists, demanding the destruction of historic symbols because they 'represent' bigoted (i.e., un-Islamic) thinking.

President Obama is implementing his own version of Sharia Law on America. Either you are a believer in the view that bible thumping, gun toting white male America is the cause of all the world's ills, or you are to be banished, politically beheaded, shamed or symbolically stoned by the sycophantic media.

My guess is that if you are a flag-flying, white male Christian conservative, you might, like me, feel a little nauseous.

Crossroads

America invented the modern day Federalist form of government when the Founding Fathers decided that no country could survive freedom if it wasn't set up to deal with a variety of needs of the people. Before the concept of representative democracy came along, the world consisted of either fiefdoms or tribal chaos. It was the Dark Ages and either you ruled by the sword or you were ruled by the sword.

The unique form of government that was begun in 1776 was essentially the idea that in order for the government to be responsive, it had to reach down to the working class. There needed to be a mechanism for people to make their needs known without making a trip to a distant or central seat of government. The idea that a more regional subset government could then manage yet another more local subset gave birth to the city, county, state model. Each subset would then interact with the next up line level to ultimately construct an overall body governing the country.

We are the United States of America because the Founding Fathers wanted there to be differences between the states. This would allow the flexibility required to accommodate the inevitable divide between human perceptions of how things should work. In any family, there will be strife. No two humans are the same and neither are their solutions to problems, let alone their prioritization of those problems.

So the solution was, if people want to, let them move to the area that best suits their way of living. Then, when a states wants to pass legislation, they can either act alone, or join with other states to make overall Federal laws. The process by which they can enact rules and regulations can vary within state legislators, but must meet tougher requirements to become national legislation.

As a basis for the individual state concept, under a Federal umbrella, was the idea that all humans are endowed by the "creator" albeit a higher authority, with certain inalienable rights that no man can 'put asunder.' These 'rights' must be respected at all levels of government because they are the skeleton of freedom. Things like freedom of speech, travel, property ownership, association and presumed innocence were so new to government that only a few people outside of the United States understood how crucial they would be to the survival of liberty from authoritarianism.

Unfortunately, in the 21st century, citizens of the US are not much better informed than those of the 17th century. Despite the near universal availability of information, many US voters are simply ignorant about freedom, the cost to acquire it, and the commitment to preserve it. Because we have enjoyed the benefits of it for 250 years, we take it for granted.

Prior to the Declaration of Independence. only the upper echelon of civilization could read. Developing any form of governance, of rule or of tribal identity was through force. There were the ruling class and everybody else. The political concept of choice hadn't been invented yet.

In America, the state is a benevolent uncle. It hands out benefits, protects the vulnerable and bestows licenses. It is a source of pride, it is the home of our institutes of advanced learning, of scientific research, of our parks and recreational facilities. It has a very comforting image, unless you are in the business of fishing without a license, or pretending to be a doctor, or trafficking in human inventory.

Other than during the Civil War, Americans have never had to defend their own home from an attack by their own government. We have not had to dethrone a dictator. We make change through an orderly and peaceful process. A process that is virtually unique on the planet.

So we are ignorant of the threats that exists to liberty.

And, even more amazing, is that the state of affairs in our country is very diverse. We integrate multiple state and national political organizations, unions, corporations and special interest groups. It is a jungle out there, so we have three tiers of government, local, state and national, designed to impose restraint, regulations and a sense of responsibility on all of us. The system is there to reign in the normal human instinct to go it alone. The old Wild West system is long gone as it was too violent and deadly, and indigenous to areas too remote or unpopulated, to sustain.

Though America has been enormously successful in distinguishing itself from the tribal chaos of the Dark Ages, in our own much more civilized manner, we do have our own turf wars always burning under the tundra. We do best when we deal with those issues locally, through our city and county representatives.

The group Black Lives Matter is an example, but as much as it hurts to see how old wounds are slow to heal, at least in America we have a process to confront the issue in a public way. Through local channels we settle issues dealing with schools, police and social services, building codes and restrictions, property rights, traffic and transportation, and human needs. Many are too big for our local organizations, so they migrate to state or national considerations.

Racial divisions are one of those issues that, as localized as much of the unrest is, is basically a national cultural issue, and will require a unified effort to fix. But upon closer inspection, the reason it has festered so long is that too many of the people involved are simply not using the system, either because they don't know how to, or because they don't want to make the effort to.

Civil illness in a free society is a result of neglect. The anger survives because the collective immune system is compromised, either by ignorance or apathy.

The state of affairs in America is at a point of distress. The human tendency to turn to tribal coalitions and internecine battles is creeping back into our national psyche. It is becoming increasingly difficult to gather clear majorities, to legislate simple, easy to follow rules that actually achieve peaceful resolutions. No matter how hard we try to bring everyone together, it seems the gulfs are growing exponentially wider.

The obvious explanation is that a generation of coddled citizens just don't want to give up anything in negotiation. They are used to being given what they want when they want it. It is extremely hard to negotiate with someone who has never had to make sacrifices, never known setbacks or deprivation. In their mind, why give up anything when you can have it all? That is because, in their experience, they have always had it all!

And by they, I mean all of us.

Now we have a difference of opinion over just about every civil issue on the table; abortion, welfare, wealth distribution and taxes, public school curricula, healthcare and home mortgage financing.

Why shouldn't undocumented immigrants enjoy all the benefits of citizenship? Why does the government need to collect data on its citizens? These are all issues that the average citizen feels are just political statesmanship and the answers are really simple, so why spend a lot of valuable video game time studying them?

It is popular and sounds so sophisticated to say, live and let live. But reality has a way of reasserting itself, often in rude ways. When President Obama said "We have Al Qaeda in retreat," he was immediately contradicted by the mass murder in San Bernardino, California.

A recent live news interview with Hillary Clinton revealed her inability to distinguish a Democrat from a socialist other than to babble about how her progressive self-characterization is all about "finding solutions." She is a presidential candidate who espouses plans to reinforce Obamacare, which places the 7th largest element of our economy under government control, to ban private ownership of guns, and yet she is unwilling to accept a mantle of being a socialist. Voters don't seem to care, probably because both Democratic candidates are pandering for votes by promising to give supporters lots of free goodies.

After suffering through several decades of intentional dumbing down of students in public schools, Democrats have made a deal with the devil;

give us your vote and control, and we will take care of your basic human needs. As a result, more and more people in America are disengaging from the duties of being a citizen, of being an informed voter, of working for a living, of providing for a family, of being self-dependent, and of supporting the country that gave them the opportunity to be so lazy.

So the American grand experiment in representative government is at a crossroads. Either we convince the average citizen that they must become better informed, more actively engaged in some level of self-governance, or we may find our state of affairs in complete functional collapse.

Border Lines

As a citizen, before we discuss a very sensitive issue, let's get one thing straight: Immigration is not the issue! The US is a nation of immigrants. *Illegal immigration* is entirely different than documented, controlled and sanctioned immigration.

To conflate, or equate, the two is simply duplicitous.

America integrates more creeds, races, religions, and natives of other countries than any other country. No place in the world has the record of embracing immigration that we have in America. This is why America is what it is, a magnet for people who want to better their situation in life.

The illegal immigration issue is about respect. R – E – S –P – E – C - T.

Respect for the Rule of Law. Either we demand it, or, as a civilization, we should expect our society and our culture to collapse entirely.

Every human being demands respect. But are illegal immigrants willing to give it? Too many, I am afraid, do not act like they understand how it is earned, and the importance to reciprocate the respect *they* demand.

We hear the word respect used in virtually every polemic about the rights of illegal immigrants.

- The human rights activists talk about the need to "respect" human dignity.
- Immigration lawyers talk about the lack of "respect" for the hardworking, tax-paying undocumented 'citizens.'
- Liberals want to eliminate racial profiling because it is "disrespectful" of our social diversity.
- The "shadow" immigrant community wants "respect" for their contributions to society, their work ethic and their family values.

Every one of the demands of activists listed above should be considered because all of them have merit and all of them would contribute to the greater good.

However, paramount above all of those claims has to be RESPECT FOR THE LAW!

Without the rule of law, which can only be attained in a free society with the full support and participation of the citizenry, none of the above can be affirmed.

When we citizens hear the complaints of illegal immigrants who have been in America for an extended period of time, and who say "I don't want to be looked at as a criminal." We want to scream, "But you are!"

You broke into our country and made yourself at home at our expense. You have stolen our tax dollars to pay for your hospitalization, your medical bills and your education. You act as though it is justified to homestead yourselves in America just because it's such a nice place to live. With that kind of logic, maybe we should all move into Bill Gates home and refuse to leave! After all, he has a great view!

OK, we left the back door open, but under the law, an unlocked door is not permission to burglarize a home! Of course many illegal immigrants are comfortable after four or five years in the US, but that doesn't make their residence here any less illegal. Every criminal who robs a bank will tell you he just wanted to make his life better.

Moving from one country to another is difficult. Many refugees lose their lives trying to escape war or violence. Those who are simply trying to improve their lot in life have good intentions. But that is not enough. Most people, given the opportunity to escape the drudgery of socialism, theocratic authoritarianism, or extreme poverty, would volunteer to take their chances in the Land of the Free. Wouldn't you?

America was founded by people with the very same intentions. We get it.

We just want you to show some RESPECT for what America stands for, the benefits and advantages we can offer you when you join our society and our unique culture. We want you to be ready to enjoy your membership as much as we do!

Historically, Americans have shed enormous amounts of blood trying to establish an environment of free enterprise and democracy all over the world. We have made heroic efforts to bring our culture of liberty to every corner of the world. That, after all, would be the best way to expand human dignity and freedom.

But the truth is, we can't allow everyone to move here. It is simply a fact of life.

Americans venerate anyone who seeks to improve their lot in life. That is the American Way. But doing it at the expense of someone else, by subverting the law, or by deceit, is simply immoral.

Most people in this country who are convicted of a crime have been working and paying taxes most of their lives, too. When a jury is confronted with proof of embezzlement, they aren't going to give the defendant much credit just because he went to church on Sundays.

So, now we know over twelve million illegal immigrants have been discovered to have broken the law. What should we do with you?

We are darned mad about all this, but there has been mitigating factors. Illegal immigrants have been providing services to many of us, which makes all of us partially culpable. Our country has reaped many benefits from their presence.

These are important, relevant mitigating factors.

But, society has an obligation to enforce its laws. We also need to make the punishment fit the crime. Putting people in jail for breaking into America is unrealistic and counter-productive. Deportation is not a viable solution for twelve million people.

So, that leaves us with parole.

Parole? Yes, a period of conditional release and supervision until the perpetrator pays dues to society for their crime. In this case, the dues are simply a period of parole while they earn their immigration rights back.

How long should the probation period last? Wouldn't it make sense to set the time to match the amount of time it takes for legal applications to be approved? Currently, that could be as long as two, three or up to ten years. There is no justification to allow law breakers to shortcut law abiding immigrants in any way whatsoever! And since they, as opposed to those in line to immigrate legally, are already here, they would be subject to paying taxes, to submitting to limited freedoms (i.e., no voting, no free medical or educational services, and restricted civil rights, such as subject to search and seizure). Why should they have access to or be rewarded with benefits those still on the outside can't receive?

Whatever it is, those who have cut in line need to wait their turn. So if it takes two years for someone playing by the rules, then Parole should start with that. In addition, as part of the penance for cutting in line, and as a token of good faith, all participants should be compelled to complete an American Citizenship Assimilation Program before the parole period even starts! That would give the educational part of the program a sense of urgency.

As a condition of parole, illegals would be required to learn English, to have a restricted driver's license, and learn to understand the Constitution of the United States of America. The program would require illegals to pass a comprehensive US history class, and to sign a Citizenship oath of allegiance. And during the parole period, all participants would have to meet all of the obligations that go along with normal citizenship privileges, such as paying taxes, and supporting law enforcement.

Of course their term could be reduced dramatically by volunteering to join our Armed Services. Successfully completing a normal four-year term in any branch would automatically earn full US citizenship.

After an illegal immigrant completes their parole period and citizenship training, we will welcome them just like we have welcomed millions of immigrants that came to our country through legal channels.

Those who refuse to cooperate should be considered felons and face immediate deportation and a lifetime ban from immigration to America. Second time violators found in the US again will be confined for a period of no less than five years and have all of their possessions confiscated. At the end of the five years, they will once again be deported. Should they be caught in our country a third time, they will receive a life sentence. Three strikes, and you're *in* for life!

Americans have kicked this issue down the road for far too long. We have reached a crossroad, and like a disillusioned family standing across our border, we all must make a choice.

Transients

The inconsistencies of our immigration laws are so glaring...

If it is illegal to sneak into the country without proper documentation, then shouldn't it follow that offering an illegal immigrant an auto insurance policy should also be illegal? Isn't giving that person, who is engaged in an ongoing illegal enterprise, a policy to protect them from liability in case of an accident with someone who is a legal citizen, aiding and abetting their crime? Does it make sense that our government encourages insurance companies to provide legal support to illegals who cause an accident and damage to persons and their property who are acting legally?

History tells us that the innocent party almost always pays an inordinate price for obeying the law, because in many cases, the illegal simply disappears and never faces their obligations. And how can that be prevented?

When determining the rate to charge teenage male drivers, insurance companies use an amortization table. It tells them the rates and nature of incidents that might qualify for damage payments. They do this to determine risk. It is called risk analysis. Consequently, most teenage male drivers pay a higher premium.

How can insurance companies accumulate data on people who live in the shadows? Do those data banks break down literacy and language rates? How many accidents are caused by people who can't speak or read English? Or never return to court? These people live transient lives, and are near impossible to document.

My point is, insurance companies, mortgage lenders, school administrators, health officials, and most public service providers cannot properly evaluate undocumented transients.

Insurance providers are being mandated to extend coverage as a political social construct, to circumvent charges of racism and xenophobia. And the direct result of these policies, that are based on smoke and mirrors, is that all of us pay a lot more, and the country is experiencing a declining respect for the rule of law.

In California, our Democratic legislature is more interested in growing and indenturing the Latino voter-base than it is in helping the rest of us to protect and grow our hard earned savings.

California's recently enacted Dream Act rationalizes spending general fund tax revenues to pay for community college tuition fees for undocumented illegal immigrants (trespassers) who were brought here before their 16th birthday. In my view, this is a blatant misappropriation of public funds, disguised as a humanitarian program to give disadvantaged kids a hand. It is indirectly rewarding the parents (or smugglers) who brought the kid into the country illegally, by providing them financial aid to attend taxpayer funded schools.

Everyone wants to help disadvantaged kids, but do we have to be dishonest and disingenuous about how we do it?

I don't see the difference between a political group giving its constituency hand-outs of public funds and giving contracts to favored interest groups in non-competitive public projects. If they gave that money to relatives, they would go to jail, but to award community college tuitions money to illegal immigrants doesn't cause a ripple on the public's radar screen?

Normally, grants, contracts, public works and maintenance program contracts are awarded through a competitive process with public scrutiny and a paper trail that provides a level of accountability. The state, for its largesse, receives something tangible in return, a new road, bridge or school building. Conversely, subsidies, poverty programs, welfare spending and other intangible investments are targeted towards an economic underprivileged class of recipients and are restricted by law to not discriminate against race, creed, sex or culture.

It is clear to me that Democrats favor these kind of "investments" of public funds, precisely because they are so vulnerable to corruption and influence buying. Having control of a state legislature gives any party a massive amount of voter groups buying power.

Though those programs are ostensibly designed to help the lower end of the socioeconomic spectrum, they also have the greatest amount of discretion, the least amount of accountability, and can gain voter approval based on their emotional appeal, while seldom proving to accomplish their stated goals (i.e., the war on poverty, the war on drugs, school busing, affordable housing, etc., etc.).

The ultimate form of misuse of public funds, it seems to me, is spending it to aid and abet an ongoing criminal enterprise. When a law abiding immigrant sees what his criminal counterpart is getting, what incentive does he have to wait in line, to work at minimum wage, to put himself through school, to assimilate into the American culture by following the recognized legal immigration process?

Just recently, California Governor Jerry "Moonbeam" Brown signed legislation to allow undocumented immigrants (trespassers) to acquire a California law degree. Therefore, it is feasible that a person living in California illegally can stand in front of a judge and jury and preach to them about how to enforce the law!

Politicians have been promising to control our borders for decades. But any unbiased review of the overall effectiveness of recent immigration legislation would have to conclude, America has no intention of controlling the invasion of our country by immigrants. In fact, the evidence points in the opposite direction: The US is encouraging illegal immigration more than legal immigration.

Is there any wonder why there are many more illegal attempts to immigrate than there are legal ones?

Jeh Johnson, the Obama appointed Secretary of the Homeland Security Administration (HSA) thinks all twelve million illegal immigrants deserve a chance to stay in the country and become full-fledged citizens, despite having clearly demonstrated contempt for our laws.

> "It is also, frankly, in my judgment, a matter of who we are as Americans," said Johnson, speaking to the United States Conference of Mayors held in Washington DC. "To offer the opportunity to those who want to be citizens, who've earned the right to be citizens, who are present in this country..."

Apparently, in his mind, successfully breaking into our country, evading ICE and acting like you belong here "earns" illegal immigrants the right to stay.

Not too long ago a woman in North San Diego County awoke to find a stranger standing at the foot of her bed. She screamed and the man bolted. He was subsequently arrested and the officer found a half-eaten quart of ice cream, taken from the woman's freezer, in his car.

Now imagine if this situation had gone like this...

> "What are doing in my house?"
> "I like your house."

> "I don't know you! Get out of my house!"

> "I deserve to be here. I am not leaving. In fact, I have already put my clothes in the bedroom closet."

> "I'm calling the Police!"

"Oh, by the way, when you go to the grocery store, buy some ice cream. I ate what was in the freezer. We're out."

Americans are out of patience with illegal immigration, with the redirection of limited resources to pander to non-citizens, and the thinly veiled efforts to build an underclass of dependents to perpetuate Democratic bureaucracies.

Tribal Anxiety

President Obama consistently reminds the world, and specifically Americans, that America is not at war with Islam. He is not alone; every major political figure has made mention of this sometime in recent history. Obama reiterates his belief that all of the anger and anti-Muslim vitriol presented in the press is not an accurate reflection of American values.

I disagree. Expressing heightened anger and rallying support for a formidable military response to a worldwide scourge of murderous, genocidal maniacs wreaking havoc on the planet is precisely in line with American values. Fighting for peace and justice is what we do. We fought against Japanese Imperialism, German Nazism, Italian Fascism, and we have and will continue to fight against fundamentalist Islamic gangsters too.

We were never at war with the Japanese people, the German or the Italian people. We were at war with their extremist leadership. Unfortunately, those leaders were using their people as pawns, and they were victimized and they suffered. Muslims are facing a similar conundrum with the Jihadist extremists. It is not up to the defenders of freedom to separate the wheat from the chaff. It is our duty to end the terror, period. It is up to Muslims to separate the peaceful from the psychopaths.

As an American, I resent Obama's barely disguised attacks on fellow Americans! Americans are not the problem in this world. Granted, Jihadi terrorists are killing and maiming thousands, if not millions, of Muslims too. Is up to the peace loving, mainstream Muslims of the world to lead the effort to rid the planet of this disease that is using their belief system to subjugate the world to some death cult ideology.

Once again, Obama appears to be talking down his nose to conservatives, and especially Evangelical Christians. He points out, " We have to understand that an attack on any faith is an attack on all our faiths."

Any faith? So a faith that delegates women to slave status, that requires death for apostates (those that do not convert), that demands believers to commit atrocities as a sign of submission to Allah, qualifies for exemption from attack?

How does that square with the Obamacare rules that require Catholic hospitals to offer abortion services or lose their Federal tax breaks as non-profits? How does that square with Obama's characterization of out of work Pennsylvanians who "cling to guns or religion or antipathy towards anyone who is not like them"? What about his administration's indifference to the FBI profiling and harassment of

Tea Party taxpayers? The most recent executive orders that schools must allow students to use restrooms based only on what gender they choose?

The list of Obama policy attacks on American's personal religious principles is endless.

President Obama, whether consciously or not, cannot avoid speaking in terms that divide Americans into tribes. And inevitably, he implies that Christians specialize in hate towards those "that are not like them." As if this universal human weakness only exists in the Judeo-Christian based American culture, and in particular, conservatives.

So his point that an "attack on any faith is an attack on all our faiths," ignores the Koran-quoting crazies screaming "Allahu Akbar!" as they run through a shopping mall, selecting innocent citizens and challenging their faith and then executing those that cannot quote the Koran. Where is his outrage when a Jihadist maniac separated the Muslims from the Christians and Jews at the San Bernardino Christmas gathering before shooting the "apostates" in the head?

I ask you, just when is he going to lecture Muslims?

President Obama could have appeared on the podium with leaders of Islam rallying their followers to take action against the threat to their belief system, families, and the very existence of America.
Either he couldn't find any, or he didn't try.

My message to President Obama: You were elected to be the President of the citizens of the United States of America, not the people of Saudi Arabia, Afghanistan or Iran. It is too late now, but it is unbelievable how shabbily you have treated 'believers' in our country. If a visitor had just arrived from Mars, he would be hard pressed to not conclude that you, President Obama, are a Muslim. And not just a mainstream Muslim, but one who harbors an enormous amount of anger towards evangelical Christians, and based on your recent policy moves, hostility towards Israel.

But Obama steadfastly claims to be a Christian though he has never publicly described his relationship with Christ. For a world leader, one who presides over the largest Christian population in the world, he sure is reluctant to show his solidarity with other Christians.

We all recall that Dr. Jeremiah Wright was Obama's Minister, the one who said, "Them Jews aren't going to let him (Obama) talk to me... he'll talk to me in five years when he's a lame duck, or in eight years when he's out of office."

Operating in the tall shadows of his sun setting administration, Obama has evidently decided he no longer needs to disguise his contempt for American Exceptionalism, Judeo-Christian centered, middle-class values and voter concerns about the hijacking of a major religion by terrorist gangsters.

His heart never was in the fight to destroy the extremist Islamic Jihad. Obama is the tribal drum beater. He never was a warrior. The only fights Obama has a stomach for are progressive political campaigns. President Obama has presided over and fomented eight years of tribal anxiety.

CHAPTER SIX

Our Rendezvous

"You and I have a rendezvous with destiny.
We will preserve for our children this, the last best hope of man on earth,
or we'll sentence them to take the first step into a thousand years of darkness. If we fail, at least let our children and our children's children will say of us
we justified our brief moment here.
We did all that could be done."

—Ronald Reagan

Stay to the Right

Watching the Republican presidential debates, I couldn't help but be concerned with the obvious impression that none of the candidates are really ready to take down Jihad. When talk show host Hugh Hewitt asked Dr. Carson the emotionally loaded question, "Are you ready to kill hundreds of thousands of people" in the War on Terror, I was outraged.

That is not a question that can be answered in the format that is allowed by the media managed debates. It is a big question with an even bigger answer. But to ask it in that fashion puts the candidate in a position of having to redefine the rules of engagement in war.

It is an important question, and it deserves a complete, nuanced response. Not just from Republicans, but Democrats too. It should be asked of all of the candidates, but in a different setting.

It points out a whole bunch of bigger issues: Is America willing to fight this war at all? Is this generation, who have been shielded from any exposure to the true carnage and human destruction of war, capable of authorizing an all-out effort to bury the enemy in ruble?

It hasn't indicated that it is.

The fact that President Obama was reelected proves that. So the question should have been, "Do you believe the voters are ready to do what it takes to win a war? Are we ready to kill hundreds of thousands of the opposition if it is necessary, and if so, as Commander-In-Chief, would you direct our military to take such serious steps to end this reign of terror in the world?"

What we are doing now is not fighting. We are executing a worldwide media optic. We are eating around the edges, making a lot of noise, taking out a few high ranking gang leaders, but you cannot call our efforts a war. Our military is so tied up with politically correct restrictions, they may as well have both arms tied behind their backs. If our military had been unleashed in Iraq, the Jihad movement would have been cut off at the knees. And, unfortunately, a lot of innocent, or at least unarmed citizens would have died, just as they did in Germany and Nagasaki.

But we wouldn't be where we are now, witnessing an unprecedented worldwide expansion of the Islamic State in the Levant (ISIL).

What worries me is that I am not sure any of the Republicans, or Democrats, are ready to take that irreconcilable step of total war. And, ergo, I am concerned that our political leaders, our "fools of engagement", are simply incapable of persecuting a winning war strategy.

Scary...

It is mid-2016 and the long and exhausting campaign for the White House is at the halfway point. We have endured dozens of Republican and Democratic debates. We see the candidates act like petulant children, screaming invective, grabbing attention, hurling insults, posing, and backpedaling a lot.

The media circus we are shown to help us determine who will be the next leader of the free world has devolved into a three-ring freak show. The whole thing is about as entertaining as watching a cock fight.

The most compelling story is Donald Trump. He only got into the race when in an offhand way when he proposed building a "world class border wall" and "making the Mexican government pay for it." Suddenly, the entire campaign dynamic changed.

The former Governor of Florida, Jeb Bush had vested his primary campaign appeal on his competency to manage a big state, to pull it out of financial collapse, and to bring Democrats into the fold. He had one hundred million dollars of campaign funds available, thinking he could save most of it to take on the presumptive Democratic nominee, Hillary Clinton.

But Trump, who admits he had no idea his proposal would have such an impact, changed everything. He hit a nerve with his politically incorrect notion that illegal immigration was unacceptable and a major threat to our nation.

The country had recently witnessed a series of unimaginable incidents of foreign immigrants crashing into our neighborhoods, bringing disease, crime and social pressures on some states that were struggling before the immigration onslaught nearly bankrupted them. The Obama administration had literally encouraged hundreds of thousands of refugees, many young children, coming from the Middle East, Mexico and Central America, with no sponsorship, no documentation, and no marketable working skills, to flood into border states with impunity.

In hindsight, Trump's spotlight on immigration was a brilliant chess move. It has had the effect of boxing out all of the other candidate's favorite subjects, forcing them into a defensive position. He grabbed the spotlight and he hasn't relinquished it since.

Interestingly, the immigration issue is far from new. In fact, it was something Jeb Bush should have been familiar with, because his brother George was haunted by it. Though George Bush is remembered for his Iraq War miscalculations, his administration struggled with immigration for eight years.

I recently uncovered a letter written to GWB in 2006. It was written by Ronald Maxwell, a Hollywood writer/producer/director, who is best known for directing "Gettysburg" and "Gods and Generals". Both films are about the Civil War. In his letter he describes in detail the extent of damage the US is suffering from the out-of-control invasion of illegal aliens.

He wrote:

> "It may already be too late to avoid a future annexation of the Southwest by Mexico." He warns the President that, "the natural weight of demographic change is accompanied by the soundtrack of racial demagoguery which seeks to legitimize and moralize this phenomenon as a 'Reconquista.'"

He goes on to characterize the Bush administration's immigration policies as captive of big business, looking for cheap labor. That he could ultimately be remembered as the President who won the war in Iraq, only to lose the war over the Southwest borders of America. He chastises Bush on behalf of the Senate, which he says shows more concern for immigrants than for American citizens:

> "The McCain-Kennedy Bill looks like it was drafted by bureaucrats at the United Nations, rather than by representatives of the United States."

Obviously, President Bush paid no attention to the Maxwell letter, in the same way that many Americans today feel that politicians have paid little or no attention to the promises made in the presidential election, or the 2014 midterm elections. Or, for that matter, since Ronald Reagan signed what was characterized as the penultimate amnesty bill, the Immigration Reform and Control Act of 1986.

The immigration issue could be the game changer in this election cycle and Donald Trump, because of his independence, his unrepentant disregard for politically correct sensibilities, and his outright anger, has placed it front and center in the 2016 race for the White House.

Historically, American presidential elections have often been determined by seminal events occurring just before the election; Dewey lost to Truman after the incumbent took a hard stand against Communism and supported strong civil rights legislation. Eisenhower defeated the heir apparent to Truman, Adlai Stevenson, running on a 'Korea, Communism and Corruption' platform.

The famous game changer 'Nixon-Kennedy' debates are credited for being a turning point in American media culture as nearly seventy-four million people watched Kennedy outshine the sickly Nixon, sending him to defeat, though only temporarily.

And we all know how George H.W. Bush dashed his chance to complete a second term when he famously said, "Read my lips! No new taxes!" then turned around and made a deal with the Democratic congress to raise taxes.

Has "The Donald" just made history by changing the terms of the election race? Can someone with literally no governmental experience, who has a tendency to make insulting and bigoted statements, who shows no recalcitrance to hammer anyone who dares to challenge his qualifications, actually maintain his momentum and eventually coalesce the splintered Republican Party to actually win the presidency?

I heard Jeb Bush stop an interviewer to say, "Hold on, I just have to get this off my chest; Donald Trump is a jerk!"

The problem with that kind of unrestrained honesty is that Jeb Bush alienated 39% of the polled Republican voters. What a strategic idiot! Condescension doesn't engender a whole lot of trust in your ability to handle world leaders, many of whom would be considered jerks by a lot of people.

Sadly, it appears he wasn't thinking at all. He was emoting his compassionate conservatism. Just the kind of confused moral certitude that has sent many Republicans home in recent losing campaigns.

While interviewing President Obama on *Comedians in Cars Getting Coffee*, Jerry Seinfeld asked him, "How many world leaders do you think are just completely out of their mind?"

Obama responded, "A pretty sizable percentage."

The facts are, a lot of people, Republicans, Independents and disillusioned Democrats are thinking, *maybe a jerk is just what our country needs right now.* We are tired of being walked all over by the Chinese, the Russians, our unions, and worse yet, we are sick and tired of watching nightly beheadings on TV perpetrated by a rag-tag bunch of international gang bangers, who are wreaking havoc using much of the weaponry we so stupidly left behind in Iraq and Afghanistan.

It feels like our esteemed, mainstream leaders are getting lead around by the nose by every whacked out special interest group on the planet.

Maybe it is going to take someone who is a lot less politically correct, a whole lot less passive, less considerate, and far less willing to look for consensus. Someone less conciliatory and much more focused on putting America back on top, unlike the current regime that seems dedicated to knocking it off the pedestal of world leadership. Someone who is assertive, pushy and arrogant, strident and positive. An ugly American.

Someone like The Donald.

I am not saying he is the only answer, but it is increasingly clear America is angry with the status quo. And mainstream politicians, like Jeb Bush, did not get traction. The Republicans have served up Bob Dole, John McCain, and Mitt Romney, and now they have followed that with several establishment types like Bush and John Kasich.

The Party worries that if a pretentious billionaire like The Donald could sweep the primaries their party would be seriously damaged. I have news for them, that party was over a long time ago.

On the Democratic side, Bernie Sanders is resonating with his rhetoric about restructuring and doubling down on the entitlement agenda; raising taxes up to 47% of income. His anti-Wall Street, free education, healthcare, and redistributionist plans are, once again, ringing true with young, disenfranchised students, minorities and poor women.

If Bill Clinton was 'The Pander Bear', Bernie Sanders is 'The Pandering Professor'.

The biggest lesson our country is learning as we suffer this water board primary season, is that we have a two party system. It has some major drawbacks, but it has proven to be effective at conserving the dream, the unique experiment in human liberty, for nearly three hundred years.

And as such, voters are forced to decide from two choices, which fork in the road they want to take.

Are we the America of Ronald Reagan, the Shining City on the Hill, with the most powerful military, the most dynamic and robust economy and the fastest growing middle class?

Or are we the America envisioned by Obama, Clinton and Sanders, a nation that requires a total overhaul of our basic Judeo-Christian system. A facial reconstruction that puts a more European look on our national identity by de-emphasizing individual ambitions and self-reliance.

Instead, emphasizing the reliance on top-down controls, programs and directions to equalize outcomes, redistribute our wealth, nationalize school curricula, promote cultural tribalism, and reduce consumer and citizen freedoms? Their vision is to end the destruction of the world's resources by government selection of energy winners and losers, equalize or even eliminate incentives for achievement, and wipe out distinguishing characteristics of gender, religion, and nationality. Do we want to rebuild America into an ideological dreamland of social and financial egalitarianism?

Do we want to reincarnate America as Orwell's *Animal Farm*?

If I look at the world stage, it becomes increasingly clear that all of the world's conflicts are essentially about the same tribal war: Communists and Socialists believe some are more equal than others and therefore the intellectual elites should be given the helm, while Islamic fundamentalists want to have a world made up of one theocratic Caliphate, where there is no wealth, no property, no business. In their ideal world, men would rule, women would serve, Allah would dish out justice and heaven would be waiting.

Across the Middle East, tribes fight like cats and dogs, just like Democrats and Republicans (but a lot more violently). The specific issues vary from tribal culture to tribal culture, but the wars are mostly about power and wealth distribution, which God should be the Commander-In-Chief, and who's camel is getting fed today.

The distribution of food and resources dictates the intensity and character of the battles, but in 2,000 years, there has never been a success story like the United States of America. So the truth is, what we fight about is relatively lightweight compared to the generational hatred and violence suffered by most human beings.

The changes our relatively benign transitions of power engender are minor compared to what Libyans, Syrians, or Somalis, Yemenis, Afghans and Pakistanis are living through.

But our children will have to live with the changes we make, especially if we boomers are unable to pass on a homeland as civilized, safe and prosperous as the one our parents bequeathed to us.

Driving While Mad

When I was a kid, my folks would occasionally argue. Usually over money. Sometimes my mom would get angry at dad because he was dismissive of her feelings and intelligence. They were best of friends, lovers and very committed to each other, but in the fifties, men were very chauvinistic and often dismissive of their wives. They were used to the leadership role, and rightly or wrongly, assumed they were better educated, more experienced, and as head of the household, entitled to make the major decisions.

But in certain circumstances, mom stepped up and complained that dad was not listening, acting condescending and implying she was dumb. When things got real heated, she would run out the back door, jump in the car, and sometimes burn rubber as she drove away. My dad would follow her out screaming "Please slow down!"

She would roar down the street, and I could see he was more worried about an auto accident than the effect of their argument. In time, she would come home, and they would make up. But not without my dad chastising her for being careless about driving while mad.

I can only imagine where she went...it is awkward to be driving real fast, emotionally disturbed, and not know where you are going...so I mention this as illustrative of where many Americans find themselves as they survey the presidential candidates for the 2016 election.

It is especially true for Republican and Independent voters who find themselves attracted by Donald Trump's totally unprecedented campaign. I contend that many conservatives and even moderate Democrats and Republicans feel like they have nowhere else to go... they feel they have been used and abused over the past decade. They have worked hard but lost ground, and the evidence indicates that the Republican party has been complicit in the demise of their lifestyle. They feel like the Democrats are now so far left that they offer no alternative, and expecting the Republicans to change is like letting your abusive boyfriend back into your bed.

So along comes a guy who says he only wants to make America great again, and that the people in charge are total morons. Yeah, that's exactly the way I feel! And since he isn't being bought and paid for by special interests, what exactly do we have to lose by handing him the steering wheel?

I can hear my dad now, "Slow down. Please don't drive mad!"

The Appointment

The appointment you have been dreading has finally arrived. After months of discomfort, illness, anger and depression, and after a long and grueling series of tests and doctor's consultations, you are just about to get the prognosis.

As you wait for the door to open and the doctor to come in, your entire life passes before your eyes. You think about all of the other times you have confronted your own mortality...that didn't take long. You never have.

You think about your loved ones, kids, wife, parents, siblings. How they seem to live in oblivion, never talking about serious illness or depression.

You remember your friend, who was struck down at a young age by cancer. Such a random and senseless loss!

The door opens....

You are the planet Earth. You have collectively decided to confront the death and destruction that is washing across the globe. You have had enough of this terrorism illness. You are now looking into your soul to ask, "Do I have cancer? Am I going to die?"

The Diagnosis

America, the leader of the free world, has been in a coma for the last decade and a half. It is just now coming off life support, but is still in very serious condition.

The doctor is standing bedside, and he is looking us in the eye. He says we have to take some responsibility for our condition, and we will be required to battle back from our injuries. We, as a nation, are still the Beacon of Freedom in the world, and as much as we have been acting like we don't know that anymore, the rest of the world hasn't forgotten. And they are depending on us, even if they won't admit it.

The doctor notes that if we capitulate to the dark forces that want us to die so they can take back the planet, if we truly aren't prepared to stand up again, to lead the good fight for liberty and human dignity, for freedom from oppression, to roll back the influences of the death culture, those people who think mankind cannot survive unless they are in charge, and unless all of us place our hopes and aspirations into their hands, then no amount of support from the doctor, from the government, or from wishful thinking will save our nation, or our planet.

He reminds us that the patient is the single most important part of the survival equation. If the patient really wants it, survival is still very possible. The patient's commitment to doing what it takes, to keeping a positive attitude, to believe in themselves and in their faith in God, is exactly what the doctor would prescribe.

In somber tones, he says he is not our Lord and Savior. He is just a messenger, a person who has the knowledge and experience to see what has made the patient ill, what efforts have been made to save the patient, and to continually assess the health status of the patient, but the doctor cannot save us.

That is something only we can do.

In immense pain, we look up at him, wondering if we have the strength and perseverance needed. The doctor smiles. He takes a long breath, and then softly, calmly, says, "I know you can do it. And so do you!"

Then, he touches his hand to his heart, and reaches out to touch our heart too. As we silently gaze at each other, a sense of warmth and energy begins to stir inside. And as the doctor closes the door behind him, we know we are now much closer to the beginning than to the end.

As the leaders of the Western world come together in recognition that they are embroiled in a war they did not start, they must overlook many issues that have divided them for generations. They are finding themselves in a battle of self-preservation. They are confronted with a sick, death worshipping cult that recognizes no authority, has no value for human life, and is willing to commit suicide at the drop of a hat if it can use it as a tool to promote its own illogical, twisted Islamic Jihad.

Watching Netanyahu, Abbas, Merkel, Cameron, Hollande and nearly two dozen other foreign national leaders lock arms in solidarity after the November 2015 massacre in Paris, was frightening, because it illustrated the seriousness of the deteriorating condition of the world.

So now the question we, along with the rest of the reluctant nations, must ask ourselves is what are we all going to do to eradicate this disease before it consumes us?

Saving Our Planet

The doctor proceeds to run down the various test results, and as he does our nation must start to think, can we be brave? Can we put up the battle it is going to take, just to give ourselves the chance to win this war? Can we beat this terminal form of cancer?

Fighting against an invisible, moving and incredibly deceptive opponent is difficult. But the first thing one must do is accept that the fight is necessary. As we sit on the edge of the proverbial examination table, what is the prescription?

So, in order of application, here is my prescription for America:

- <u>Officially Declare War on the Cancer</u>: Just like any disease, and especially a disease like cancer that is extremely good at disguising itself, leaders of the civilized world, have to come to grips with the reality of having a potentially terminal illness. Radical Islamic Jihad is in our body. To have any chance of surviving, we must make a decision to fight it with every ounce of energy in our collective soul.

- Hire the Best Oncologists: We must expand our intelligence and strategic military capabilities exponentially. It is due or die now; either we win this battle or there will be no more battles to fight. When you get attacked from behind, you must fight with reckless abandon; win first, ask questions later. America must consult and recognize the expert's advice on treatment; bar no expense, and embrace all effective strategies.

- Change Our Diet: We must stop feeding ourselves politically corrected and filtered news, rosy scenario strategies, and Orwellian assumptions and tell the truth. Stop using political-speak to tell the patient lies about their future survival prospects. It is counter-productive to suggest that we should just keep acting like nothing is wrong. Americans, and all civilized nations, mustengage in the fight for life and demand sacrifices and commitments of ourselves.

- Monitor Progress and Demand Compliance: Our allies must step up and take responsibility for a share of the costs, both physically and financially. When an ally stumbles, America must be prepared to exact a cost. The US military must demand access to any battlefield at any time, or deem offending countries as hostiles. All for one, and one for all.

- Apply Strong Doses of Radiation/Chemo Therapy: In war, if you have a superior weapon, use it! If nuclear or even chemical weapons would be effective in extenuating circumstances, we should not hesitate to use them. Our enemies know we have these capabilities but are playing on our reluctance to use them. It's too late to play nice. Does anyone really think Jihadi maniacs will not use those same weapons should they get their hands on them?

- <u>Stop Acting Scared</u>: It is demeaning and demoralizing to constantly complain about the situation we find ourselves in. Grow up and get real. When we act terrified, we are encouraging our enemy. In WWII, those that whimpered and cried, that refused to contribute, were universally shamed and pushed aside. When your foxhole is being overrun, there is no time for equivocation.

It is time to conscript all levels of the media, news, entertainment, and communications to develop messages to drive home to all age and interest groups how important it will be for them to help shape the future of our planet.

The fact that President Obama considers climate change more threatening than Islamic Jihad is astonishing. If the world does not totally vanquish the threat of this death cult, there will no planet left to save from pollution.

We need to reassert our language. We have allowed the terrorists to define their own image. The media calls them insurgents, radicals, extremists, Taliban, anti-establishment rebels and any number of Orwellian distortions. These monsters don't deserve anything more than terminology that accurately describes their state of being; they are thugs, mutants, demonic agents of hell, mass murderers and mentally depraved enemies of mankind.

Drop the idea that they are terrorists, because as of now, the whole world is working together to eliminate them from our planet. They are not terrorizing us; they are coalescing us. Instead of tearing us apart, they are bringing us together. Besides, terrorist is their name for themselves. I say they are swine.

When George Bush famously said after 911, "Either you are with us or against us" he was pilloried by the left. They said he was inflaming the terrorists, causing undecided Muslims to join the radicals. That his cowboy mentality painted the philosophical conflict in absolutes of right and wrong, leaving no consideration for shades of grey, and therefore forcing many otherwise morally upright people to disrespect America.

That kind of moral equivalence is disgusting and stupid. It assumes every person is rational, and only when provoked by insensitive moralism would suddenly become an inhuman, cruel and fatalistic maniac. Bush was right. He may not have been particularly adept at verbalizing the situation, but just like politics in America, when we are confronted with war, there are only two choices...the good guys or the bad guys.

Remember the WWII German citizen Martin Niemoller?

> "First they came for the socialists, and I did not speak out— because I was not a socialist. Then they came for the trade unionists, and I did not speak out— because I was not a trade unionist. Then they came for the Jews, and I did not speak out— because I was not a Jew. Then they came for me—and there was no one left to speak for me."

It is time to own up. Either you believe in liberty and the freedom of dissent, the freedom of the press, the freedom of worship, and the right to self-determination, or you don't. Why is it so hard to pick your team? Do you want the dark side to win this war?

Here are some other aspects of my prescription: People who counsel, comfort, or mingle with the enemy will be prosecuted. Period. Governments who provide, directly or indirectly, support or refuge to the enemy, will be subjugated. Period. Businesses who in anyway conduct commerce with the enemy, will be dissolved and their assets seized and used to support anti-terrorism expenses. That includes multi-national corporations. Period.

In war, we must ignore border restrictions of our fighting forces. We would never have won WWII if we had to show passports at the beaches of Normandy.

It is time to be a civilized human or choose not to be. It will be necessary for all of us to stand up and be counted, one way or the other. Those that can be shown to collude with known affiliates of Islamic Jihad will be dealt with harshly as they are all *accessories after the fact to crimes against humanity*. They are the very definition of war criminals.

The idea that injuries and death among innocent civilians when drones bomb Jihad leadership meetings must be rejected. Using civilians as shields is a strategy. The people who are not wearing uniforms are no less responsible for the acts of the militants; they are in collusion. If they are hostages, then they will not survive anyway. Let it be known that the strategy of hiding behind the skirts of women will not save anyone from aerial annihilation. As with radiation treatment, there can and will be collateral damages. It is the cost of fighting a war that has already progressed to this degree. Had we been more forthright in stopping this back when Palestinian, radical Islamist agents kidnapped Israeli Olympians, we might not have to be so aggressive today.

In locking arms, we are saying we know we are in trouble, but we are willing to go the extra mile to assure our values and freedoms are protected for our children and their children. We must look at the big picture, the planet Earth!

We have the physical and digital resources to monitor the ecosystems of those believed to be supporting Jihad. We must share the intelligence, coordinate the campaigns and work as a team, or we will find ourselves returning to the Dark Ages. To stop mutant cells from duplicating themselves, we need to cut off their oxygen, choke them to death by denying them their lifeblood, be that food, resources, weapons, money or safe haven.

The one most important element of this worldwide effort is leadership. The United States of America has traditionally been the default Commander-in-Chief of anything of this size and scope. Unfortunately, under our current situation, it is clear our Commander-in-Chief either is incapable, or worse, unwilling to accept the responsibility to step up to the plate and reach out to other foreign leaders, to define the enemy, to rally the people, and to take command.

President Obama's half-hearted, recalcitrant leadership is ripe for exploitation by the leaders of Jihad and their slippery, phony political puppets who pretend to align with the defenders of freedom. So we must look elsewhere.

We need an alpha male to be in charge.

As for all of us regular, working class citizens just trying to make ends meet, it means we, the people, are going to have to step into the void and with a worldwide street level series of demonstrations, civil unrest, boycotts, strikes, and all of the grass-roots programs developed and perfected by the disillusioned, disenfranchised, and underrepresented activists of the sixties and since, must now redirect our energies to demanding a coordinated effort to promote the survival of civilized mankind.

It is up to us to make it COOL to stand up for freedom. It is up to us to remind leftists, moderates, uninformed, ignorant and apathetic people that they need to get involved. It is going to be especially ugly for those people if the freedom of expression, the freedom of choice, of ambition, of self-determination and civil rights, is overrun and destroyed by Islamic fanatics.

Some cancer patients survive the disease. Many do not. Those that pretend it is not present in their bodies, universally succumb, mostly sooner rather than later.

Not too long ago, the Pakistani school where Jihadi animals slaughtered 150 schoolchildren and their teachers, was reopened. A

15-year-old student, Ahmed Nawaz, who was seriously wounded but managed to survive the attack, delivered a message to the world; a message we can only wish our President would have had the guts to deliver after the San Bernardino slaughter...

The kid proclaimed, "We are not scared of you."

This should be the theme for our WORLD WIDE WAR ON JIHAD!

Recalculating America

Let me summarize some of the ideas and issues I have raised and why I think a national turn to the right is a critical political and cultural recalculation at this juncture in our history.

There has been a movement inside of our country, most of which has been directed by academia, to push America to the extreme left. To slowly bring the 'toad to a boil', and to eventually kill our capitalist-oriented Democratic republic form of self-government in favor of a top-down, statist-style government.

The who, what, where and why, are not as important as it is to realize these forces are acting in a unified method and are as determined to end our way of life as we are to preserve it.

The places where these struggles take place are, beyond the battlefields of the Middle East. They are here, in our schools, our conventions of civilization such as traditional marriage, gender roles, election processes, and our legal system, our Judeo-Christian morals, our unified language, our borders, our history and the role of the media.

Make no mistake, this is a worldwide trend, with America as the target, because where America goes, so goes civilization.

Our people are being divided into tribes and pitted against each other, on purpose. Our political system is under assault by disgruntled Islamic religious extremists and their naive ideological subordinates, the extreme left. Our enemies are clandestine and asymmetrical, some of which are outside influences, but most of which are homegrown "useful idiots."

Our individual freedoms are rapidly eroding, our national security is a vacant promise, our relationships with our leaders are near extinct and suspect at best.

Our children, having been exposed for most of their youth to experimental and substitute parenting, and to academic and digital brainwashing, now find themselves lost in space without so much as a tether to reality, are turning against their elders and most conventional wisdom at alarming rates.

The tenor of our daily lives has transformed into an endless narrative of childish fixations on media stimulation, superheroes, sports and entertainment, celebrity, and diversions of extreme self-aggrandizement, drugs and narcissism.

The multi-tentacle media is fixated on the gruesome, the profane and the lure of a devolved and depraved range of entertainment.

Our language has coarsened, our civility is gone, and our politics are purposely obtuse and beyond dirty.

The current political arena and the presidential campaign is a reflection of all of these sickening devolutions of our once great country. The entire spectacle indicates a desperation beyond anything since the opening of World War II when President Roosevelt said, "The only thing we have to fear, is fear itself."

As always, we should put our challenges in proper perspective; we are not the first generation to confront massive, seemingly impossible social, economic and political mountains to climb. Mankind itself is a phenomenon that defies science and reason. Each moment that civilization survives is against all of the odds. However, what is different is the absence of the iconic American can do attitude so synonymous with our predecessors.

I believe that we all need to recalculate our relationship with our homeland. Our destination is on the right. We have allowed our national attention to be directed too far left.

Our pledge of allegiance was to pass on a world of opportunity, of diversity, and of stability. To do that, we need to look to a "higher authority" to recognize just how lucky we Americans are, how important our existence is, and what a challenge Americans face to protect and to nourish this precious experiment in human existence--this unique social construct designed to promote liberty and justice for all.

This awesome, and still tenuous thing called America.

EPILOGUE

"Nothing is more wonderful than the art of being free,
but nothing is harder to learn how to use than freedom."

— Alexis de Tocqueville, *Democracy in America*

America's Magical Stuff

Sometimes we hear that it is America's wealth and arrogance that motivates terrorism. The use of asymmetrical weapons like suicide bombers is rationalized as the only way poor, repressed peoples can make war on great Satan nations like America. The goal, the apologists say, is to wreak chaos on the underlying institutions of their enemies, which will force them to address their grievances and, ultimately, lead to a redistribution of America's amassed wealth and privilege.

This asymmetrical warfare strategy, as implemented by organizations such as ISIS or Al Qaeda, can with relatively small amounts of cash and resources, exact tremendous damage to the economic infrastructure of the international business community and its geopolitical centers of power.

Osama Bin Laden rightly claimed that his attack on the World Trade Center in New York on September 11, 2001 began a decade of economic decline for the dominant economies of the Western World. Since that time, we have seen financial markets of the US, Japan, China, and Western Europe gradually slow, and as in 2008, come close to total collapse. And the trend has continued to reach across continents to affect nearly all of the European and Western economies that have built their strength through growing interdependency and trade relationships.

Though it is too complex of an issue to tie all of this economic turmoil to the 911 attacks, it is not unrealistic to look at the overall trend since that milestone, and recognize that the whole world changed on that day.

Even if we simply look at the 911 attacks as symbolic, they delivered a very clear message: the terrorists put a silver dagger into the heart of the symbol of the world trade cabal that represents everything that is evil to Islamo-fascists. They didn't pick the World Trade Center, the Pentagon, and presumably the Capital Building, or perhaps the White House, by accident. The Jihad attack was directed at the soul of America.

Unfortunately for them, however, is the fact that America's strength is not just monetary. It is not a result of its ownership of real estate, or the gold held in its bank vaults.

It is ironic that the Islamo-fascists, many of whom are of Arabic descent, are falling victim to an illusion. Like the classic Oasis in the desert, our great financial wealth looks more alluring and seductive from a distance, than it actually is. To those who have little tangible wealth, and the implied power that is associated with it, it appears to be the elixir of life.

Like so many laws of nature, humans are slow to recognize the law of unintended consequences. The Al Qaeda attack on the Twin Towers, though intended to disrupt the US economy, disturb the American psyche, and to ultimately weaken America's worldwide power and influence, may in the end, have had exactly the opposite effect.

How? Simple...

The premise that America's power and influence was rooted in its wealth was wrong to begin with. To the contrary, our strength comes from America's Magical Stuff. It is something intangible, something invulnerable, something no measure of evil, no amount of violence or bloodshed can destroy.

Our immutable strength is so far removed from the trappings of wealth; the terrorists have not yet recognized how unassailable it really is. It truly is Magical Stuff, and were the terrorist successful at extinguishing it, they would plunge the world into the dark place it was before the advent of civilization. But that can't happen.

This Magical Stuff is innate to the American culture. It grows in the environment of enlightenment. It is invisible, has no shape, no body, no physical properties to which acts of terror can cause damage.

It is, however, recognizable within many uniquely American endeavors. It is easily detectable within our music and art. In fact, it resides in all creativity, American or otherwise. You will find large amounts of this stuff in humor, humility, and humaneness, all of which is absent in the dark world of the death culture of terrorism.

Americans spread this Magical Stuff around, wherever they go, which makes waves in the Sea of Intolerance where terrorism breeds. And when the Americans are absent, the Magical Stuff lingers, haunting the purveyors of anger and resentment.

What is the Magical Stuff we speak of? Why can't an army of terrorists, or any military force ever hope to conquer it? What is the Magical Stuff that has fueled the ascendency of modern industrialization, advanced communications, the exploration of space, and liberated millions of people around the world? What force is it that has advanced human knowledge to create remedies for pandemic diseases?

It is the SPIRIT OF FREEDOM.

There has never been a time in history when it didn't exist. And though America didn't invent it (God did), we did create a garden where it could flourish. And as a result of the creative juices it unleashed, the rest of the world has had exposure to it. It is called a spirit, precisely because it comes from the heart, not from the earth.

The SPIRIT OF FREEDOM outlives individuals and governments. It is immortal.

The unintended consequences of the terrorist attacks on the World Trade Center made it abundantly clear that though you may cause pain and suffering to the People of America, it will only strengthen Americanism.

The concept that all men yearn to be free, is like the sun. You can create darkness in places, but you cannot extinguish the energy or the light the sun emits.

No matter what should become of the wealth of America, people worldwide can count on Americans to protect and nurture the SPIRIT OF FREEDOM and that the sun will rise every day.

— Rick Elkin

www.ingramcontent.com/pod-product-compliance
Lightning Source LLC
Chambersburg PA
CBHW050113280326
41933CB00010B/1078